T0037066

POTIONS

POTIONS

a guide to cocktails, tinctures, tisanes, and other witchy concoctions

nikki van de car

illustrated by anna godeassi

RUNNING PRESS
PHILADELPHIA

Running Press
Hachette Book Group
1290 Avenue of the Americas, New York, NY 10104
www.runningpress.com
@Running_Press

Printed in China

First Edition: August 2022

Published by Running Press, an imprint of Perseus Books, LLC, a subsidiary of Hachette Book Group, Inc. The Running Press name and logo is a trademark of the Hachette Book Group.

Print book cover and interior design by Susan Van Horn.

Library of Congress Control Number: 2021952286

ISBNs: 978-0-7624-7873-6 (hardcover), 978-0-7624-7875-0 (ebook)

1010

10 9 8 7 6 5 4 3 2 1

contents

INTRODUCTION
the craft's cocktails

WHAT MAKES A POTION A POTION?

Well, it's not ingredients like eye of newt or toe of frog, since nobody actually ever used those things anyway. Those were just code names witches employed for regular old plants. Eye of newt? We call that mustard seed. And that frog's toe we've heard so much about? It was just a buttercup.

When it comes to potions, what makes the concoction so magical is not the ingredients at all.

A potion is about *intention*—just as all magic is. When you imbue your ingredients with meaning and focus your will on a desired outcome, you are working magic, and you are brewing a potion. Your personal power is what brings forth that magic.

Think back to when you were a kid: you probably made incredibly efficacious potions using random leaves and drops of dew. And a non-witch could make every single recipe in this book and still not brew a single potion.

Not all potions are meant to be consumed (after all, buttercups are poisonous), but the mixtures in this book are all meant to *taste good*, and make you *feel good*. Among these enchanted offerings, there are kombuchas, tisanes (which is just a witchy name for herbal teas), tinctures, infusions, boissons (aka mocktails, but, seriously, nobody likes that word), and *absolutely* cocktails.

Witches have been incorporating alcohol into their rituals and potion-making for centuries. Libations are traditionally poured to honor loved ones who have passed, for example, and frankly, alcohol is the best way to draw out the essential properties of various magical herbs. Consider absinthe, a distillation of wormwood, which if consumed in unsafe quantities produces visions. That's certainly not recommended, but it does speak to the history and efficacy of alcohol in magic, which goes back centuries. In ancient Rome, Egypt, and China, herbs were steeped in alcohol to enhance spiritual connection . . . and the same principles hold true today.

Our current fad of playing with craft cocktails makes it that much more fun to incorporate *the* craft into our lives, and we'll explore many different ways to do so in the pages that follow. Every recipe you'll encounter will include a brief ritual of some kind, whether setting an intention, using a crystal, or invoking sun magic or moon magic. You'll also find longer rituals scattered throughout that will support your overall magical practice.

This book is organized by the intention—the magic—behind each recipe: you'll find sections covering Creativity, Calm, Love, Courage, Balance, Harmony, Protection, Wisdom, Intuition, and Growth, and each will contain a variety of recipes to support that intention. Often, we seek out magics that can aid us in a particular area, whether through manifestation, rituals, or spellcraft. But sometimes, what we seek is instead a *type* of remedy—a particular variety of potion that can satisfy a craving or spark the imagination. If that is the case for you and you're looking to choose between kombuchas rather than set a specific intention, the index will point you in the right direction.

As you bring these magical ingredients and the intentions you set with them into your body, maintain an open heart and mind, allowing for whatever comes to you. Let the experience unfold, and pay attention to how your perspective and your perception of events change. That is how the magic happens.

CRYSTALS, MUDDLERS & SHAKERS

There are certain supplies every witch—especially one with designs on brewing potions—must have on hand. You'll need a lot of glass jars in a variety of sizes and a place to store them. If you have space under your sink, that will work, as will a shelf in the back of a cupboard. Some of our tinctures need to steep for quite some time, and they'll have to be kept out of the light to allow the magic to sink into them undisturbed.

You'll also need some barware basics to aid in preparing your ingredients and witchy concoctions:

SHAKER ◆ You don't have to get really fancy here—I know a witch who used an old baby bottle as a cocktail shaker. Even a glass jar will do. But when you're working with ice, the shaker can get really cold, so it doesn't hurt to have something insulated on hand. Using a shaker will also make straining your finished drink a lot easier.

JIGGER/MEASURING CUP ◆ The recipes here will give measurements in ounces, so you can either use a small measuring cup—make sure it goes down to half an ounce at minimum—or a double jigger, with measurements down to half an ounce at minimum.

VEGETABLE PEELER ◆ You'll be using this to make twists of citrus for garnishes. Simply peel off a strip of lemon, lime, or orange rind.

MUDDLER ◆ You can use the pestle from your mortar and pestle, or even the back of a wooden spoon.

glassware

Using specific glassware is definitely optional—as always in magic, it's not what you use, but the intention behind it that counts. But incorporating these vessels does make brewing your potions, especially the cocktails, more fun! There are many, many more specialty glasses than are listed here, but these six will see you through.

MARTINI GLASSES ◆ A classic for witches and non-witches alike, martini glasses are ideal for cocktails and concoctions served straight up (without ice).

COUPE GLASSES ◆ This glass is technically optional, as straight-up drinks can be served just as easily in a martini glass . . . but they're a little less messy, as the rounded bowl keeps the drink from spilling. And they certainly add an enchanted quality to all of your finished brews.

COLLINS GLASSES ◆ These are used for drinks with added seltzer or kombucha.

ROCKS GLASSES ◆ Anything served with ice but without seltzer is ideally suited for a rocks glass.

WINEGLASSES ◆ Many of the recipes you'll find in the pages that follow incorporate wine, and you may also enjoy some of the boissons in wineglasses.

CHAMPAGNE GLASSES ◆ These glasses are also optional, but *very fun* when you're drinking something pretty and sparkling. Remember: using the tools around you to enhance your mood and intention is a type of magic all its own and can be a powerful addition to your practice.

crystals

More than just pretty rocks, crystals are naturally formed molecular structures that resonate with certain kinds of energy. The following crystals are good to have on hand at all times, and they will be incorporated into certain rituals for preparing various potions.

AGATE ◆ For courage and strength.

AMAZONITE ◆ For intuition.

AMBER ◆ For strength and clarity.

AMETHYST ◆ For intuition, calm, wisdom, and tranquility.

APOPHYLLITE ◆ For calm and harmony.

AQUAMARINE ◆ Reduces fear and tension.

AVENTURINE ◆ For growth.

AZURITE ◆ Soothes and invites calm.

BLACK TOURMALINE ◆ For protection.

BLOODSTONE ◆ For courage and vitality.

CALCITE ◆ Amplifies energy and boosts creativity and intuition.

CARNELIAN ◆ For harmony. Also enhances creativity and courage.

CHRYSOCOLLA ◆ For wisdom.

CITRINE ◆ For creativity.

CLEAR QUARTZ ◆ For calm, harmony, wisdom, and all-purpose healing.

GARNET ◆ For creativity and strength.

GREEN AVENTURINE ◆ For love, and the courage to pursue it.

HEMATITE ◆ For protection.

IOLITE ◆ For balance.

KYANITE ◆ Enhances psychic ability.

LAPIS LAZULI ◆ Amplifies thought, enhances psychic ability, intuition, and wisdom.

MALACHITE ◆ For love, particularly self-love, and harmony.

MOONSTONE ◆ For calm and harmony.

OBSIDIAN ◆ For protection.

OPAL ◆ For creativity, intuition, and to enhance psychic ability.

PEARL ◆ For balance.

PERIDOT ◆ For energy and positivity.

PYRITE ◆ For protection and grounding.

RED JASPER ◆ Boosts internal fire.

ROSE QUARTZ ◆ For love of all kinds.

RUBY ◆ For creativity.

SAPPHIRE ◆ Invites wisdom.

SARDONYX ◆ For courage.

SELENITE ◆ Clears negative energy.

SMOKY QUARTZ ◆ For protection, and to invite creativity.

SUGILITE ◆ Sparks intuition.

SUNSTONE ◆ Invites positive energy.

TIGEREYE ◆ Boosts personal power.

YELLOW JASPER ◆ Helps maintain internal balance, supporting growth.

magical plants

In the recipes, rituals, and spells that follow, you'll be called to use many different magical plants, from herbs to fruits and even flowers. Using the bounty of Mother Earth in our spellcraft is part of a time-honored tradition, and it will allow you to magnify the power of your own magic.

AGAVE ◆ For growth.

ANISE ◆ For intuition and growth.

APPLE ◆ For love and wisdom.

BARLEY ◆ For courage and balance.

BASIL ◆ For harmony.

BLACKBERRIES ◆ For wisdom.

BLUEBERRIES ◆ For wisdom.

CACAO ◆ For love.

CALENDULA ◆ For intuition.

CARAWAY ◆ For courage.

CHAMOMILE ◆ For calm.

CHERRY ◆ For intuition.

CINNAMON ◆ For wisdom and growth.

CLOVE ◆ For harmony.

COCONUT ◆ For balance.

CORN ◆ For creativity.

CUMIN ◆ For creativity.

ELDERFLOWER ◆ For harmony.

FENNEL ◆ For courage.

GINGER ◆ For courage and growth.

GRAPE ◆ For creativity and love.

GRAPEFRUIT ◆ For growth.

JUNIPER ◆ For love, protection, and intuition.

LAVENDER ◆ For calm, balance, and intuition.

LEMON ◆ For balance and growth.

LEMON BALM ◆ For harmony.

LIME ◆ For wisdom, intuition, and growth.

MINT ◆ For courage, balance, and growth.

MUGWORT ◆ For creativity and intuition.

MULLEIN ◆ For balance.

OAK ◆ For wisdom.

ORANGE ◆ For creativity and growth.

PARSLEY ◆ For courage and protection.

PEPPER ◆ For protection.

PINE ◆ For protection.

POTATOES ◆ For harmony and protection.

RASPBERRY ◆ For creativity and protection.

RHUBARB ◆ For love.

RICE ◆ For growth.

ROSE ◆ For love.

ROSEMARY ◆ For wisdom and growth.

SAGE ◆ For wisdom.

STRAWBERRY ◆ For harmony.

SUGARCANE ◆ For love.

THYME ◆ For courage.

WATERMELON ◆ For growth.

YARROW ◆ For protection and intuition.

COCKTAIL COMPONENTS

Many of the recipes in the chapters ahead make use of base components: think of them as the building blocks of the magic you're creating through your potions. Beyond utilizing these ingredients in the recipes and spells that are outlined here, you can work with them to riff on crafting your very own cocktails, and explore from here!

bitters

Bitters are used to flavor a variety of cocktails, and are, in fact, a tincture—which is a rather fancy word that simply means herbs steeped in alcohol to extract flavor and magical properties. They are quite potent, and so only a small amount is required at any time. Because of their strong taste and mystical significance, bitters are an ingredient in several of the boisson recipes, making them not strictly nonalcoholic—though very little alcohol is used.

The bitters recipes included here use vodka, but you can also try brandy or any other high-alcohol spirit when brewing your own. There's no need to go super high-quality for your base, as the flavor of the spirit is intended to be overwhelmed by the herbs. Steep your bitters for at least two weeks in a dark place, occasionally shaking the jar in which they're kept. Make sure you label your jars, or you may end up altering a potion in a way you don't intend!

When using bitters, most cocktail recipes call for a "dash"—which amounts to just a little less than a milliliter. That's easy enough to measure out when you're using commercial bitters and the bottles come with those handy plastic dashers (that's actually what they're called). If you have leftover bitters bottles, you can decant your homemade bitters into them, but if you're measuring from a jar, the best thing to do is use an eighth of a teaspoon, which amounts to about two-thirds of a milliliter. The recipes that follow will call for an eighth of a teaspoon for one dash, a quarter teaspoon for two, etc. If you keep your bitters in the jar you made them in, just make sure to store them in a cupboard out of direct sunlight; they will continue to develop their flavor.

infusions

Infusions are lower-potency tinctures, and creating them will follow a similar process to the one you'll use for their more intense cousins. The amounts for infusions, though, is where things diverge. The intention here is for your infusion to be a more significant part of the potion—most often a cocktail—rather than just a small dash of flavor and magic. The ratio of spirit to herb is higher, and the steeping time is shorter—most often, only three days will be necessary, though you can always steep for longer if desired. The longer they steep, the more the flavor will develop, so take care to strain them before they get too overpowering! When you're using fresh herbs, make sure you wash and dry them first.

simple syrup

Some of the infusions will be for simple syrups, a basic mixture of sweetener and water that will come in handy for many of the brews that lie ahead. A basic simple syrup is one part water to one part sugar. If you'd like to keep extra on hand or you're making a large-batch recipe, feel free to increase the quantities below.

1 cup water

1 cup sugar

All you need to do is warm the water in a saucepan, stirring in the sugar until it has dissolved. Don't let the water boil or it will evaporate too much of the liquid and change the ratio of sugar to water. Simple syrup will keep in the refrigerator for two weeks or so.

shrubs

In cocktail parlance, a shrub is an acid-based component that adds flavor and brightness. They also allow us to bring the essence of magical herbs and spices into our potions without needing alcohol. With shrubs, the energies and properties of these plants can be mixed into beverages that are better for, say, the middle of the day. Historically, shrubs were consumed in the 15th century as medicinal cordials—a practice that continued in Colonial America. You can play around with reducing the level of vinegar in this recipe—and with adding other fruits—but the basic blend is as follows.

1 lemon

¼ cup white sugar

¼ cup mild vinegar, like white wine or champagne vinegar

Slice the lemon thinly, crosswise. Place the slices in a jar and sprinkle the sugar over them, shaking to coat. Allow the slices to cure in the sugar for one hour, then add the vinegar. Let the jar sit for three days, out of direct sunlight, somewhere you'll see it and give it your attention and intention. Shake it occasionally, then strain. Store them in either a dark-colored glass bottle or in a cupboard. Shrubs will keep for two to three weeks.

basic kombucha

Brewing your own kombucha is a simple and rewarding process, one that truly evokes the feeling of being a witch conjuring forth something *from* nothing. *In brewing kombucha, you will grow and care for your* SCOBY *(short for symbiotic culture of bacteria and yeast)—a living creature that will facilitate the fermentation of your ingredients. The process of making your own kombucha is also incredibly versatile, and you can add different flavors to each batch, as you'll see later. All this magical process requires is a bottle of store-bought kombucha to begin (the flavor doesn't matter), some black tea, and some sugar.*

½ cup store-bought kombucha

4 bags black tea

½ cup sugar

Reserve the last half cup of your store-bought kombucha and set it aside. In a large saucepan, bring 7 cups of water to a boil. Turn off the heat, then steep four bags of black tea in the liquid (you can change to green tea or even herbal tea later, once your SCOBY has grown good and healthy), and stir in half a cup of white sugar until it dissolves. Let your sweet tea come to room temperature, then pour it into a large jar. Add your reserved kombucha, and cover the jar with a dish towel, sealing it with a rubber band around the rim of the jar. This will allow for airflow, while keeping out any unwanted visitors.

Let your kombucha brew in a dark, cool place for three to four weeks. During this time, the beneficial bacteria in the kombucha will feed off of the sugar and caffeine, forming a colony on the top of the liquid in the jar. This is your SCOBY, and it's a little like a rubbery Frisbee.

This first batch of kombucha will be too vinegary to drink—but you can use all but half a cup of it for cleaning. Remember, witches are resourceful! Once you've gone through your initial batch, this will be your process whenever you are brewing kombucha:

1) Wash your hands before touching the SCOBY, and set it aside on a plate while you pour out the brewed kombucha, taking care to reserve half a cup of liquid for your next batch. Pour your kombucha into another jar, and add any flavorings you like. (You'll find many suggestions, organized by intention and type of magic, throughout the chapters that follow.) Seal your container with a cap and let it steep in the refrigerator for one week to enhance the potion's flavor and promote carbonation. After the week is up, taste to see if it's ready, then enjoy! When you're ready to drink your kombucha, you can strain it into a glass. The kombucha will continue to gently ferment in your refrigerator, so it's best consumed within a week or two.

2) Meanwhile, to begin your next batch, bring 7 cups of water to a boil. Remove the water from the heat, stir in half a cup of sugar, and steep four bags of black tea. Let the mixture come to room temperature.

3) Add your sweet tea to your reserved kombucha, and carefully tip the SCOBY back into the brewing jar. Cover the jar with a dish towel and seal it with a rubber band. Let it brew for 7–10 days.

alcoholic kombucha

None of the recipes in this book call specifically for alcoholic kombucha. That said, it's quite easy to brew and serves as a slightly healthier alcoholic cider. Allowing your kombucha to reach this stage will help it to transmute even further, shifting from a mere drinking vinegar to something that will draw out the powers of the herbs used to flavor and enchant your kombucha even more.

½ cup sugar

½ cup warm water

¾ teaspoon dehydrated champagne yeast (available online)

To boost the alcohol content of your finished brew, you'll simply put the kombucha through a second round of fermentation. Dissolve the sugar in a half a cup of warm water, then stir in the dehydrated champagne yeast. Let the yeast start to fizz and activate, then pour the mixture into your decanted kombucha.

Let your kombucha brew at room temperature for another one to two weeks, though this time you'll want to loosely cover it with its lid, rather than a dish towel. (The idea is to let some pressure out, so your brew doesn't explode, but not too much air in.) Taste for sweetness and alcohol content, and when your hooch booch is at the level you want, it's time to add flavorings and allow it to carbonate in the refrigerator, just like with regular kombucha!

SCOBY MAINTENANCE

Eventually, your SCOBY will get too thick and rubbery, and your kombucha will start to taste a bit vinegary as a result. When this happens, simply strip off the top few layers of your SCOBY. You can throw them away, but they make nice gifts for fellow witches who don't want to have to brew a SCOBY from scratch, as well.

You'll also want to keep a close watch on your SCOBY. If it starts to develop black or green mold spots or becomes infested with fruit flies, you'll need to toss it and start over. You can work to avoid this by protecting your SCOBY—both with your intentions and by taking care that it is covered with a dish towel to prevent outside particles from entering the container.

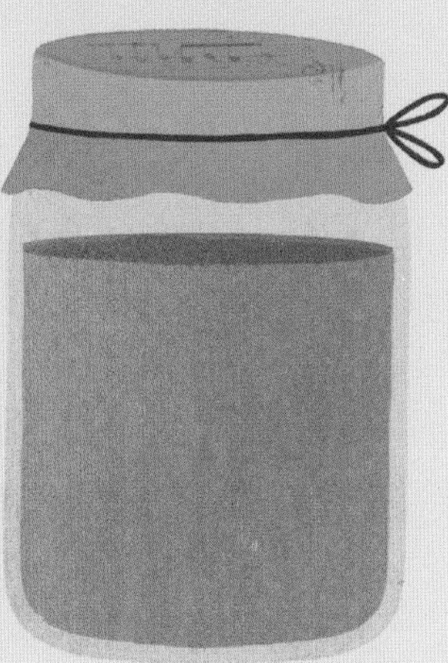

CREATIVITY

CREATIVITY IS THAT BURST OF INTEREST, enthusiasm, and, yes, magic that can spring from deep inside of you. It is one of the most joyful intentions we witches can conjure, and the following potions will help spark *your* creativity. If you're feeling a little stuck, a little uninspired, or even just in need of a little boost, dive into these potions. The cocktails you'll find in this chapter feature corn-based bourbon or wine, as both are associated with fertility—and what is creativity but fertility of the mind and soul? Other ingredients you'll find include orange, cumin, and raspberry, which promote inventiveness while also stimulating growth and protecting that budding spark. The crystals you'll fine most useful are opal, garnet, carnelian, calcite, citrine, and smoky quartz.

creativity bitters

Use these bitters to imbue your magical intentions for creativity into a tiny, concentrated package, then include them in your cocktails, boissons, and more for a boost of enchantment.

1 orange

¼ teaspoon cumin seeds

1 teaspoon dried mugwort

¼ cup vodka

Begin by peeling half an orange with your vegetable peeler. Pop the peels on a baking sheet and roast at 200°F for an hour. When they're done, place them in a jar and top them with the cumin seeds and dried mugwort. Cover with a quarter cup of vodka and shut tightly. Let your tincture sit in a cool, dark place for two weeks, surrounded by your chosen crystals for creativity (see pages 5–6 for suggestions). If you like, first press your crystals to your sacral chakra, the energetic source of your creativity, imbuing them with your energy. Every few days, shake your steeping jar, and as you do, infuse the tincture with your intentions for creativity. What are you hoping to spark?

orange creativity shrub

This shrub is meant to provide energy and growth to your creativity, allowing it to expand from a spark to a bright flame.

1 orange

¼ cup sugar

¼ cup white wine vinegar

Slice half an orange thinly, then place the slices in a jar. Sprinkle the quarter cup of sugar over them, then close the jar and shake it vigorously, coating each orange slice with sweetness. Put some energy into this, knowing that this vigor will result in a blaze of creativity. When you feel complete, set the jar to rest on your counter or table in the sunshine if at all possible, so that the light and warmth of the sun will invite even more fire. Surround your jar with crystals, perhaps even placing them in a grid or pattern, with the jar at the center.

After an hour, add the quarter cup of white wine vinegar and let the mixture steep for three days and three nights. If you can, leave the jar in the center of your grid to further draw on the magical properties of your crystals. If that is not an option—for not all witches live in places with vast space—simply put it aside somewhere, perhaps leaving a crystal or two close by to boost the shrub's energetic vibrations. Shake your jar occasionally, always with that same vigor. On the morning of the fourth day, you can strain out the liquid—it's ready for use.

creativity tisane

If you are able to forage raspberries, you can gather your own for the Raspberry Kombucha for Creativity (see page 22), and you can also collect some raspberry leaves for this herbal tea. Fresh, young raspberry leaves are high in antioxidants and contain vitamins B-12, D, and E, as well as magnesium, copper, selenium, and zinc. But if you can't find fresh raspberry leaves, dried leaves are available at most health food stores or online. The kind of creativity raspberries invite is the slow, patient growth of creation. Raspberries sprawl and protect their own potential, waiting to produce the fruit of their labors until they have established a foundation that can support them. This is what we need, sometimes—creativity with structure.

1 cup fresh, or 1 teaspoon dried, raspberry leaves

Honey, to taste

If you're using fresh leaves, you'll need one full cup's worth; with dried leaves, you'll need only a teaspoon's worth in a tea strainer. Heat a kettle of water, and let it come to a boil. Turn it off and let it rest for three minutes, then pour it over your tea leaves. Let them steep for 10 minutes, covering your cup with a small plate to keep it from losing too much heat. Strain your tea or remove the tea strainer, and stir in some honey to taste. Stir clockwise to invoke the movement of the sun, and imagine that stirring sensation moving within you, invigorating whatever may have become stagnant.

When you feel ready, carry your tisane over to your favorite chair, and take out your journal. As you sip, write down whatever comes to mind—anything at all! It could be a free association lists of words, a recounting of a dream you had the night before, a memory not-quite-forgotten . . . anything at all! The idea here is to let the warmth of the tea uncurl whatever has been clenched up within you, releasing a wellspring of magical creativity.

SUN RITUAL FOR CREATIVITY

For this ritual, you will wake up with the sun. If that's not your ideal way to start the day, you're not alone—but consider that when you're trying to birth something, to create something, the time to do that is at the moment when the world is waking up . . . when it is being reborn and creating itself anew.

If you can go outside and find a place to watch the sun come up, absolutely do so, but if not, just pick out a good quiet place to sit. Indoors, it will likely still be quite dark, so light a candle at the moment the sun comes up, letting your small fire help you connect to the fire of the rising sun. The world is waking up, just like you. Stretch your arms above your head, roll your neck, and give a great, big yawn. Breathe in the fresh oxygen, and breathe out whatever has been stagnant within you.

This is a new day. What will you bring to it?

raspberry kombucha for creativity

Your Basic Kombucha can serve as a launchpad for so much magic. Utilize the living, breathing energy of kombucha and infuse it with even more wonder through plants and crystals that ignite your creativity.

1 batch Basic Kombucha (see page 12)

1 cup raspberries

1 orange for zesting

At Step 1 of the Basic Kombucha process (see page 13), add the raspberries to a jar large enough to hold both them and your 7 cups of kombucha. (If you don't have a jar that will work, you can use two jars, but you'll want each to be quite full; if they've got an inch or more free space at the top, your kombucha won't be quite as carbonated.) Smash the raspberries with a wooden spoon to release their juices, setting your intentions for releasing your own creative juices as well. Add a few gratings of orange zest, visualizing what you wish to spark as you grate. Decant your kombucha into this jar and seal it tightly. If the organization of your refrigerator allows, place a smoky quartz atop the jar, and let it rest in the fridge for one week—don't shake! At this point, your kombucha is busy carbonating and bubbling, and you want to protect that process. Prepare your next batch of kombucha to keep that SCOBY happy.

When the week is up, carefully unscrew your jar. Taste your kombucha—is it ready? If so, strain it again into a fresh container, whether it's one left over from store-bought kombucha, an empty wine bottle, or a clean jar. You can mix your kombucha into one of the boissons in this section or enjoy it as is whenever you feel the need for a sparkling burst of insight.

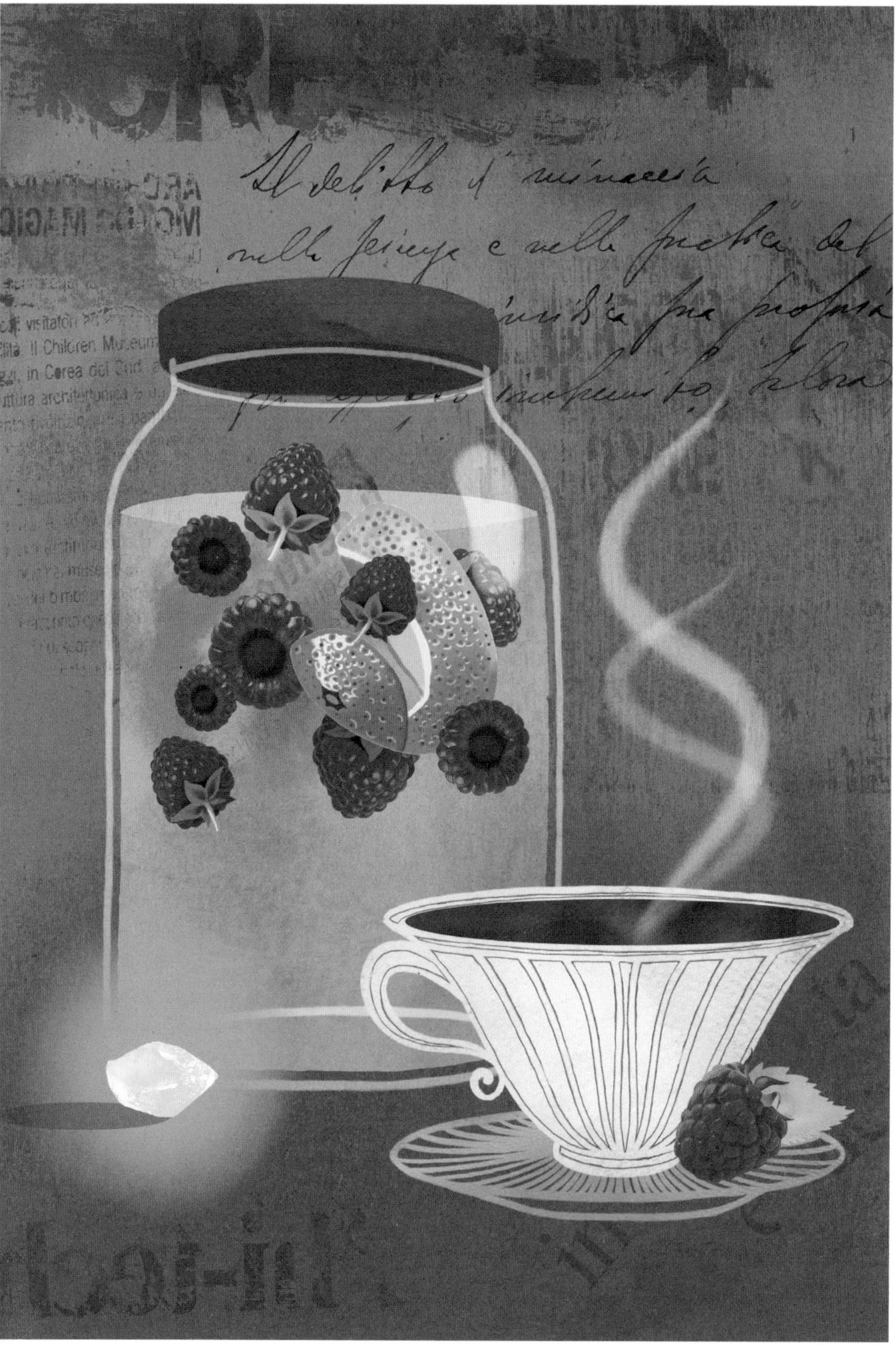

witchy cointreau

This first infusion recipe is the most complex you'll encounter in this book, but it's also very rewarding. You're crafting a versatile orange liqueur, one that can be used in a variety of cocktails, including the margarita, the Sidecar, the Cosmopolitan, and the Mai Tai. By creating it yourself, you're brewing a potion that does more than just add flavor—it adds your own power as well, bringing your flavor and intention to everyone you serve it to.

For this recipe, you'll make and use dried orange peel by peeling half an orange and roasting it at 200°F for an hour (see page 18).

Dried orange peel, from half an orange

1 tablespoon fresh orange zest (from the other half of the orange)

½ cup brandy

½ cup vodka

2 cloves

1 cup Simple Syrup (see page 10)

As with the Creativity Bitters, you'll begin with dried orange peel. When the peel is ready, place it in a jar and add the fresh orange zest, brandy, and vodka. Shake well, again being as vigorous as you can to show your commitment to your own creativity. Let the jar rest in a cool, dark place, surrounded by the appropriate crystals. Allow it to steep for one lunar cycle, shaking occasionally. At the last night before the end of the cycle, add the cloves. Let your potion steep for one more night, then strain. Stir in the Simple Syrup. Shake vigorously one last time—maybe even dance with your jar! Let that creativity flow.

fresh start raspberry mint spritz

This refreshing sparkling drink brightens the mind, giving you a burst of energy and innovation. The mint sprig invites clarity, as well, which can help if you've been feeling stuck. We'll dive into this creative potion in two parts: first with a raspberry syrup and then in the assembly of the finished drink.

FOR THE RASPBERRY SYRUP:

1 cup raspberries, fresh or frozen

½ cup sugar

½ cup water

FOR ASSEMBLY:

Sparkling water

A sprig of mint

White wine (optional)

Bring the ingredients for the raspberry syrup to a slow boil on the stove, then let them simmer for 30 minutes. Stir occasionally, moving clockwise with the sun, and bash up the raspberries a little, helping them to break down and release their juices. Strain out the syrup, collecting the brilliant red liquid and allowing its vibrant hue to arouse your own creativity. You can save the stewed raspberries and use them as a jam, if you like. Let the syrup cool completely before using. Your raspberry syrup will keep in the refrigerator for four to six weeks.

To make the spritz, add 1 ounce raspberry syrup to a collins glass filled with ice, and top with sparkling water, adding more syrup to taste. Garnish with a mint sprig, and spike with white wine if desired. Sip on a sunny day, while working on a project that inspires you.

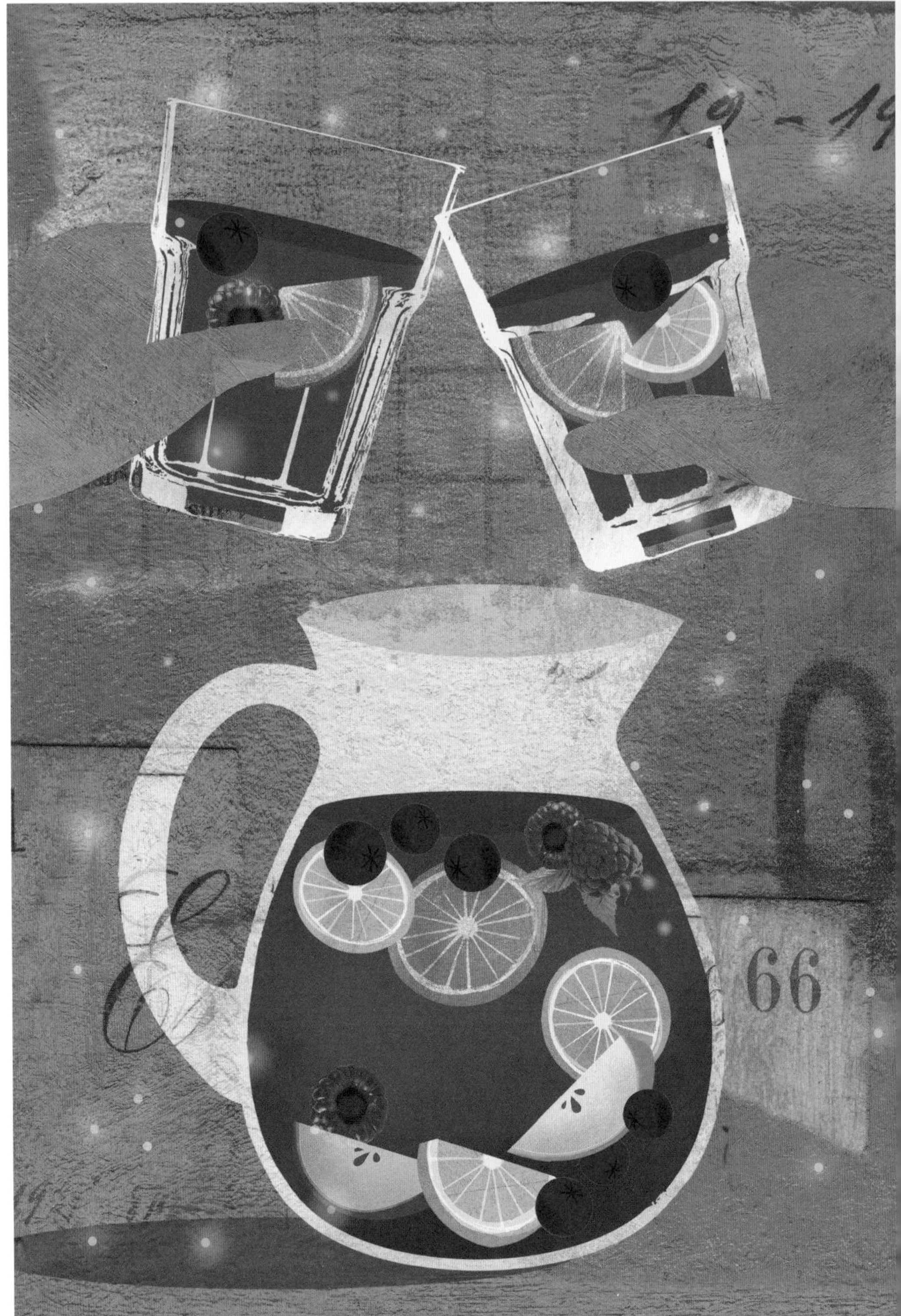
66

creative sangria

According to legend, Bacchus, the Roman god of hedonism and creativity, drank a whole lot of wine. And so it is in his honor that we partake of this sangria, a heady mixture of fruit and red wine. In tapping into Bacchus's mindset, we draw on ideas of ancient magic and possibility, which can elicit our own new ideas and release our inhibitions. Traditionally, sangria calls for a Spanish wine like Rioja, and you can add whatever fruit you have on hand—apples, lemons, oranges, peaches, and berries.

1 bottle dry red wine

3 ounces Witchy Cointreau (see page 24)

1–2 ounces Simple Syrup (see page 10), to taste

1 cup Raspberry Kombucha for Creativity (see page 22)

Add all the ingredients to a pitcher and serve over ice. Share with friends and laugh together, enjoying life.

raspberry orange creativity boost

This potion harnesses both raspberries and oranges to give you a burst of vitamin C, which will get those creative juices flowing and give you the energy to follow wherever they lead.

Raspberry Kombucha for Creativity (see page 22)

1–2 teaspoons Orange Creativity Shrub (see page 19)

2 dashes (¼ teaspoon) Creativity Bitters (see page 18)

Vodka or red wine (optional)

Pour yourself a collins glass of Raspberry Kombucha for Creativity over ice, then add the Orange Creativity Shrub and Creativity Bitters. If you like, you can spike it with a splash of vodka or red wine, and sip it while you sketch, write, paint, or simply daydream. Allow your creativity to flow, feeling the support of the energy of orange and the nurturing inspiration of raspberry—they will hold you and help you as you drift wherever your explorations take you.

creativity old-fashioned

This is a classic recipe, with a little twist—which frankly is often all we need to infuse something with our magic and make it our own. You can personalize anything with just the slightest tweak—a practice that will help you get started on any project when you feel you have nothing new to offer.

1 teaspoon sugar

2 dashes (¼ teaspoon) Creativity Bitters **(see page 18)**

Twist of orange

2 Luxardo or maraschino cherries

2 ounces bourbon

Splash of seltzer

Muddle the first four ingredients in a rocks glass. Add ice and the bourbon and splash in the seltzer. Give it a stir and enjoy while putting your own spin on an old idea.

CALM

THESE POTIONS ARE INTENDED TO HELP YOU find peace in a stressful, anxiety-ridden world. There isn't always much we can do to block out the stressors in our day—traffic jams happen, work deadlines loom, and family obligations are inescapable. But we can support ourselves, developing ways to stay serene even in the midst of the storm.

It seems fitting that the herbs we will turn to for these potions are simply chamomile and lavender. Those two are the powerhouses of calm, and their flavors blend together remarkably well as they support and soothe us. We will also draw on the power of crystals to enhance our tranquility. Moonstone, azurite, and aquamarine will help us breathe more easily, while hematite can keep us grounded.

calming bitters

Chamomile and lavender can settle and soothe you, letting you release whatever you have been carrying—even if you're only putting it down for a moment. They are supported here by a gentle burst of lemon, so that you have the energy to get up again after taking advantage of the rest offered by chamomile and lavender's calming vibrations.

1 lemon

1 teaspoon dried chamomile

1 teaspoon dried lavender

¼ cup vodka or other neutral spirit

Begin by peeling a lemon with your vegetable peeler. Pop the peels on a baking sheet and roast in your oven at 200°F for an hour. When they're done, allow the peels to cool, then place them in a jar. Add the dried chamomile and dried lavender. Cover the mixture with a quarter cup of vodka and shut tightly. Let your tincture sit in a cool, dark place for two weeks, surrounded by your chosen crystals for calm (see pages 5–6). If you like, before you place your crystals around the jar you can cup them in your palms and breathe on them gently, exhaling all that causes you anxiety, allowing them to disperse any energy you don't want. Every few days, swirl your bitters. Don't shake hard, just give them a gentle stir. Set your intentions for peace and quiet.

calming lavender shrub

Draw on the grounding properties of lavender in this refreshing yet balancing shrub.

1 lemon

1–2 teaspoons dried lavender

¼ cup sugar

¼ cup white wine vinegar

Thinly slice one lemon, then place the slices in a jar. Sprinkle the lavender on top, followed by the sugar, then close the jar and shake it, coating each lemon slice with sugar, before setting the jar to rest on the counter. Surround it with your choice of calming crystals, placing them carefully and with intention and invoking peace and quiet as you set each one down. You might even press each crystal to your root chakra first, helping you to feel safer and more grounded. Let your crystals infuse the lemons with their calming energy for an hour, then add the quarter cup of white wine vinegar. Let this sit for three days and three nights. If you want to, put it in a protected place, perhaps beneath the leaves of a houseplant or resting on a beloved book. Give it a gentle shake from time to time, but nothing too strenuous.

On the morning of the fourth day, strain out the liquid. It's ready for you.

lavender-infused vodka

This infusion is very simple. It imbues the relatively blank slate of vodka with the subtle, aromatic flavor of lavender. You don't need to use your top-shelf vodka for this, as the flavor will be altered, but the smoother the vodka the better, because the lavender won't steep for quite as long as it would when you are making a tincture.

2 tablespoons dried lavender

4 cups vodka

Place the dried lavender in a jar, and cover it with the vodka—please note, you can adjust that ratio as you choose, so if you want to make less lavender vodka, use 1 tablespoon of lavender to 2 cups of vodka. Swirl the lavender around, and then place the jar in a cool, dark place, keeping a calming crystal close by, for three to seven days, tasting it occasionally until it has the flavor you are looking for. Use this brew to bring calming energy into your cocktails, drawing on the magical essence of this restorative plant.

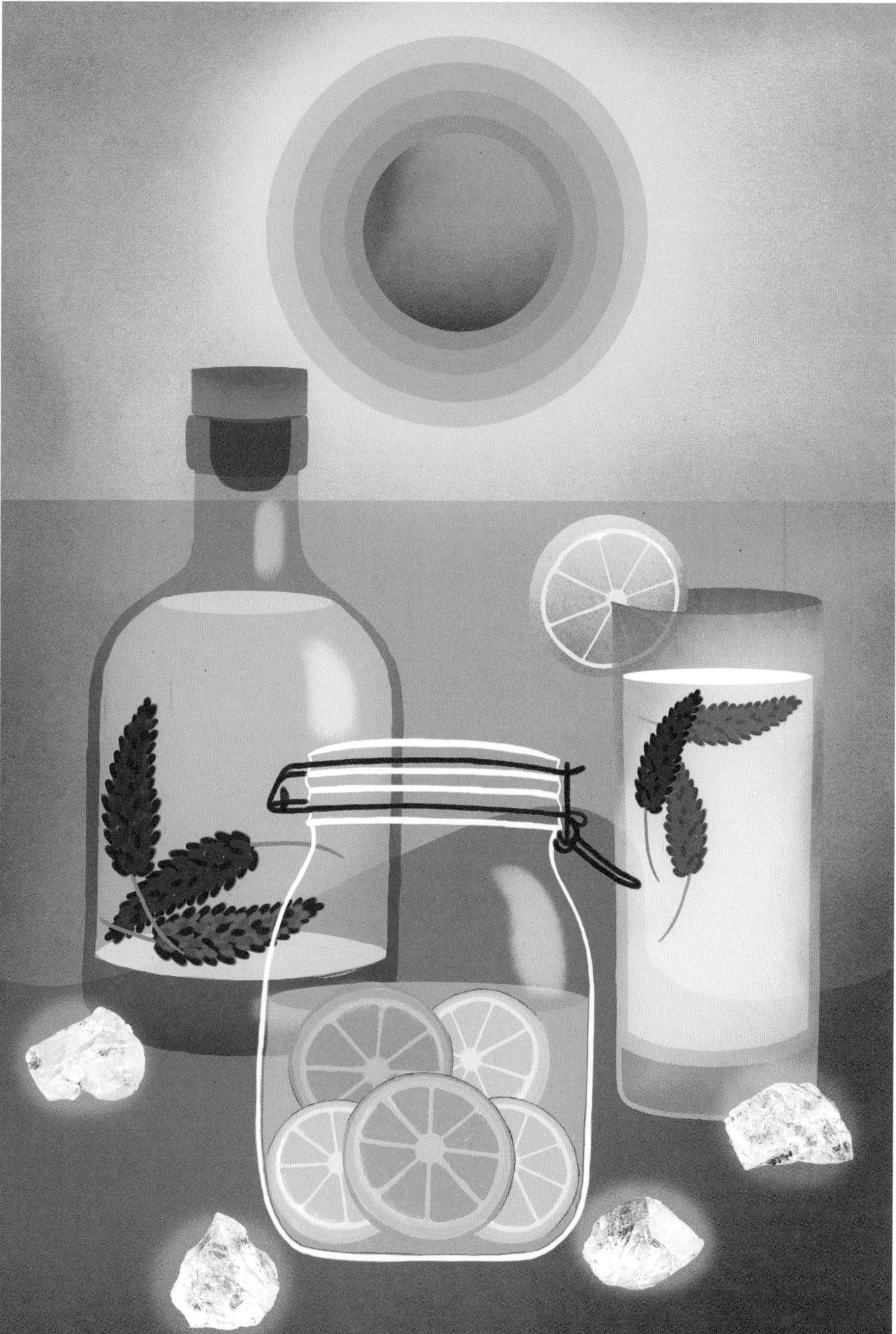

calming tisane

This herbal tea is ideal for any time when you need to just take a moment and sit. When your heart is racing and your anxiety has spiked, don't allow yourself to spiral—go put on the kettle and brew some calming magic.

½ teaspoon dried lavender

½ teaspoon dried chamomile

1 teaspoon honey, or to taste

Milk, to taste (optional)

Put a kettle filled with water over medium-high heat and bring to a boil. Meanwhile, add the dried lavender and chamomile to a tea strainer. When the water has boiled, turn it off and let it rest for three minutes, then pour the water over your tea strainer into your mug. Cover it with a small plate and let it steep for at least five minutes.

This does mean that it will take anywhere from 15–20 minutes from the time you recognized that you needed a cup of tea to the moment when you actually get to enjoy that cup of tea. Use that gap to begin to disengage from whatever has been impacting you. If you're in the middle of an argument, explain that you need to take a break. If you're stuck in a problem with work, set it aside. And if you're just anxious for no reason, know that this is totally normal, too. Spend the time while your tea is brewing taking slow, deep, even breaths. Recognizing your own needs and addressing them—through changing your environment, engaging in meditation, or the like—bring their own kind of magic, as you own your feelings and make peace with the wave of your emotions.

When your tea has finished steeping, stir in a teaspoon or so of honey. Add a splash of milk, if you want it, and slowly blend your tea by stirring widdershins, or counterclockwise. At the same time, mentally unwind whatever is knotted up within you. Carry your tea to a comfortable, quiet place to sit (or as quiet as possible), and inhale deeply before you take your first sip. As you enjoy your tea, take care not to stew over whatever was distressing you. Instead, listen to the rain, snuggle a pet, or read a good book. Allow yourself to relax.

CALMING RITUAL

Sometimes, the best thing we can do for ourselves is to go lie down. If you can get outside to lie flat on the grass or under a tree, absolutely take advantage of what nature has to offer. But if that's not an option, just go find a place to get as low to the ground as possible. Lie on the floor if you can or wherever you can feel at peace and sense the foundational magic of Mother Earth. (Don't let looking for a space remind you of chores left undone—there is no judgment here!)

Let yourself feel the pulse of the earth beneath you. All that is happening to you has happened before. Tempers have been lost, mistakes have been made, and feelings have been hurt. That doesn't make what you're experiencing right now any less real or less painful, but sometimes it can help to remember that you have already been here and made it through. Our experiences and emotions—and the experiences and emotions of everyone else in the world—both good and bad have seeped into the earth beneath us. Mother Earth can and does hold it all.

Lie in her arms, and know that you are safe there. Let her hold you, just for a moment, so you can remember that you don't have to hold everything and everyone all the time yourself. Release the weight of your body. If it helps, scan your whole body in stages: relaxing your toes, then your feet, then your ankles, and so on, all the way up through every part of you. Feel the air—and essential element in magic and life—as it brushes over your skin. When you are ready, let your sense of that air begin to wake you back up. Let it pull you up to your feet, so that you can carry on, knowing that you are always supported.

calming lavender chamomile kombucha

The struggles we navigate out in the world on a daily basis are often also experienced internally, in our gut—that place where our emotions churn. This kombucha is a healing tonic, a potion to calm those roiling anxieties.

1 batch Basic Kombucha (see page 12)

2 tablespoons dried lavender

2 tablespoons dried chamomile

At Step 1 of the Basic Kombucha process described on page 13, decant your 7 cups of kombucha into a jar or jars, leaving just a little space at the top of the jar to boost carbonation. Sprinkle a total of 2 tablespoons of dried lavender and 2 tablespoons of dried chamomile over the kombucha. Do this gently and with intention, as if you are sprinkling a sense of lightness and well-being. Seal the jar and swirl it gently to mix the herbs. Prepare your next batch of kombucha, while allowing this soothing batch to rest in the refrigerator for one week. At the end of the week, carefully unscrew the lid, and take a taste. If the flavor and carbonation levels are where you want them to be, strain your kombucha into bottles. If not, let it sit for a day or two longer, resting peacefully.

cold-brewed sparkling tea

This relaxing beverage also turns on our two star ingredients, but we are preparing it slightly differently from the potions that have come before. Cold-brewed tea is very easy; it just requires a little advance planning—as so much magic does.

2 teaspoons dried lavender

2 teaspoons dried chamomile

Honey, to taste

Sparkling water

Vodka (optional)

Add the dried lavender and dried chamomile to 2 cups of still water. You can either mix them directly in the water, or use two separate tea strainers—just one will pack the herbs in too tightly and they won't diffuse properly into the water. Cover the container and pop it into the refrigerator to steep for 6–12 hours.

When it's ready—or when you have need of it!—stir in some honey to taste and top it off with some sparkling water, perhaps with some vodka to spike it. Sip it slowly as you let your shoulders drop and your heart rate settle. Feel the sparkles on your tongue descending into your body, an effervescence that is dissolving any tension you are holding and blowing it away like bubbles on the breeze.

a soothing london fog

A traditional London Fog involves mixing Earl Grey tea with steamed milk and is usually served sweetened. It is a very soothing drink already, but in this case, we're going to bring it down even more—because, while delicious, Earl Grey does contain caffeine, and that's the last thing you need when you're feeling anxious. Allow the natural, mystical properties of calming herbs to take this beverage to a place of pure serenity.

1 batch Calming Tisane (see page 36), modified

½ cup milk of your choice

2 teaspoons honey

¼ teaspoon vanilla extract

Gin (optional)

Brew up a cup of the Calming Tisane, but make it twice as strong by using only half the water. Meanwhile, heat up half a cup of milk. (You can use the microwave, but try not to scald the milk—you want it quite hot, but never boiling.) When your tea has steeped, add your milk, honey, and vanilla extract. You can also spike this with an ounce or so of gin, if you like. Let its soothing, gentle warmth and magical herbs relax you like a hot bath.

lavender collins

This is about as peaceful and herby as a drink can get. It's meant to be sipped on a rainy summer afternoon, while you read a good book or work away on a hobby you enjoy.

1½ ounces Lavender-Infused Vodka (see page 34)

Calming Lavender Chamomile Kombucha (see page 38)

1 lemon, divided into one wedge and one slice

A sprig of lavender

Pour the Lavender-Infused Vodka into an ice-filled collins glass. Fill to your desired level with Calming Lavender Chamomile Kombucha, then add a squeeze of lemon. Give it a good stir, and garnish with a sprig of lavender and a slice of lemon.

As you sip, focus your energies inward. Feel the path of the sparkling lavender as it moves through your body, down your throat, and into your belly, activating your solar plexus chakra. Sense it grounding you as you release all your tension into the earth below you.

calming toddy

This riff on a hot toddy uses chamomile tea rather than plain hot water, allowing you to draw on the magical properties of this famously calming flower.

1 teaspoon dried chamomile

2 ounces whiskey

2 teaspoons honey

2 teaspoons lemon juice

¼ teaspoon Calming Bitters (see page 32)

Put a cup of water on to boil, turning it off when the first bubbles start to appear. Steep the dried chamomile for five minutes (you could use lavender as well, but the flavor doesn't work quite as well with whiskey). When your mug of tea is ready, stir in your remaining ingredients. Sip this whenever you're not feeling at your best, either physically or mentally. Let it help you to tap into your inner reserves of calm to reset and start again.

LOVE

WHEN WE TALK ABOUT WANTING MORE LOVE in our lives, we mean *all* kinds of love—romantic love, sisterly love, friendship, the love for the children in our lives, and the list just keeps unspooling. And it's not just about the love we receive, but also the love we have to give. When life gets challenging, we can feel a lack of love moving in either direction, so that we don't sense it being given (even though it is) and we don't notice that we are giving any of it away (even though we are). These potions will help you tap back into that love—the love that is already there, moving and flowing to you and from you, always. And most of all, it will help you find the love within yourself. Self-love can often be the hardest to feel, but it is the most important and magical love of all.

Unsurprisingly, chocolate, apple, and rose are three ingredients used most often to invoke love. Juniper and grapes also have a magical history in love spells, so you'll see cocktails in this chapter that contain gin and wine. (Sugarcane is one more so you can also experiment with rum.) These recipes also include rhubarb, that tart, bright red vegetable, which according to legend the infamous witch Baba Yaga would employ to increase the potency of her love spells. You can support your spellwork with rose quartz, malachite, and green aventurine.

loving bitters

This simple bitters recipe has a light, delicate flavor, sure to enhance feelings and intentions of love.

1 teaspoon cacao nibs

1 teaspoon dried rose petals

¼ cup vodka or brandy

Combine the cacao nibs and dried rose petals in a jar. Cover with a quarter cup of vodka or brandy. While we often use vodka for its neutrality, you may opt for brandy in this instance, since it is a fortified wine and grapes enhance love magic.

Shake vigorously, but with a kind of tenderness—you want to put some energy into this, but you also want to be loving. Let your tincture rest in a cool, dark place for two weeks, surrounded by your chosen crystals (see pages 5–6), but visit it often, tending to it with that loving energy.

potent rhubarb shrub

This shrub won't rely on citrus, as rhubarb has plenty of tart flavor all on its own. The bright red of these stalks will diffuse into the shrub, promoting passion and intense connection.

1 stalk rhubarb

¼ cup sugar

¼ cup white wine vinegar

Slice the rhubarb stalk into half-inch chunks and place them in a jar. Sprinkle a quarter cup of sugar on top, then close the jar and shake it to coat each red chunk in sugar crystals. Place rose quartz, malachite, or green aventurine atop and around your jar, sealing in the loving energy you are bringing to this potion. If you like, press the crystals to your heart or your lips before you place them, whispering your intentions.

After the rhubarb has rested for an hour, add the quarter cup of white wine vinegar. Let your shrub steep for three days and three nights, and on the fourth day, decant it. This will make for an intense shrub, so a little will go a long way—but isn't that the kind of love we want to feel?

rhubarb-infused simple syrup

Rhubarb simple syrup is a bright, glorious red, with a powerfully tart flavor, but it is still sweet enough that it brightens a drink, rather than overwhelming it. Use this in the love potions that follow.

1 cup chopped rhubarb

½ cup sugar

Chop a cup's worth of 1-inch rhubarb chunks, then place them in a saucepan. Add the sugar and a half cup of water, and bring to a simmer. Let the mixture stew over very low heat for 30 minutes, stirring occasionally. Allow your instincts to guide your motion here. Do you want to stir clockwise, in the direction of the sun? This will help you share your love with others. Or would you rather feel more love within, finding affection for the aspects of yourself that might be shadowed or secret? In that case, stir widdershins or counterclockwise, and let that motion begin to unfurl what you're holding so tightly.

When your syrup is ready, strain it out, pressing against the rhubarb chunks with your wooden spoon to get all the syrup out. The stewed rhubarb makes for delicious compote, served either with goat cheese or stirred into yogurt or over ice cream.

juniper rose kombucha

This kombucha is layered with flavors and intentions, offering you ample opportunities to infuse loving intentions and mindful magic into your potion.

1 batch Basic Kombucha (see page 12)

2 tablespoons dried roses

2 tablespoons juniper berries

At Step 1 of the Basic Kombucha process described on page 13, decant your 7 cups of kombucha into a jar or jars, leaving just a little space at the top of the jar to boost carbonation. Add a total of 2 tablespoons of dried roses and 2 tablespoons of dried juniper berries to the kombucha. (You can find these either online or at some health food stores.)

As you add your roses, think about the gentle sweetness of love, the sense of peace and comfort it can bring. Think about how treasured love can make you feel and the way you treasure others—and yourself.

As you add your juniper berries, think about the brightness of love. Those who truly love us can see things about us we hide from everyone else, including ourselves. And those we truly love value what we have to give them. Giving and receiving love energize us, bringing a sense of lightness and joy.

Seal the jar, and swirl it gently to mix your herbs together, blending the complementary sides of love. Prepare your next batch of kombucha, as you allow this loving batch to rest in the refrigerator for one week. At the end of the week, carefully unscrew it, and take a taste. If the flavor and carbonation levels are what you want them to be, strain your kombucha into bottles. If not, let it sit for a day or two longer.

LOVE SPELL

Bottle spells are an old form of hoodoo magic, a spiritual practice created by enslaved Africans in the South and the Caribbean. This bottle spell is not hoodoo proper, but it is inspired by it. Use an empty bottle or jar, and begin by placing small items in it that represent the kind of love you want to invite into your life. You might add a feather to represent a light, fun love. You might add an acorn to symbolize a love that will grow strong. Or perhaps you could write your specific intentions on a piece of paper, fold it up toward yourself three times (or a multiple of three), and then place it in your jar.

Once you've added your desired items, pour honey over them—just enough to cover—then add some red wine to fill the jar. Seal it and shake it well, coating all the items with honey and wine.

Place a small candle, like a tea light or votive, atop your jar. Anoint the sides of the candle with ylang-ylang, jasmine, rose, or patchouli essential oils, and gently rub a drop of the same oil over your heart. Light the candle, and then stare at the flame, allowing its fire to spark your heart. Allow the intentions from within your jar to drift up into the candle and alight within you as well.

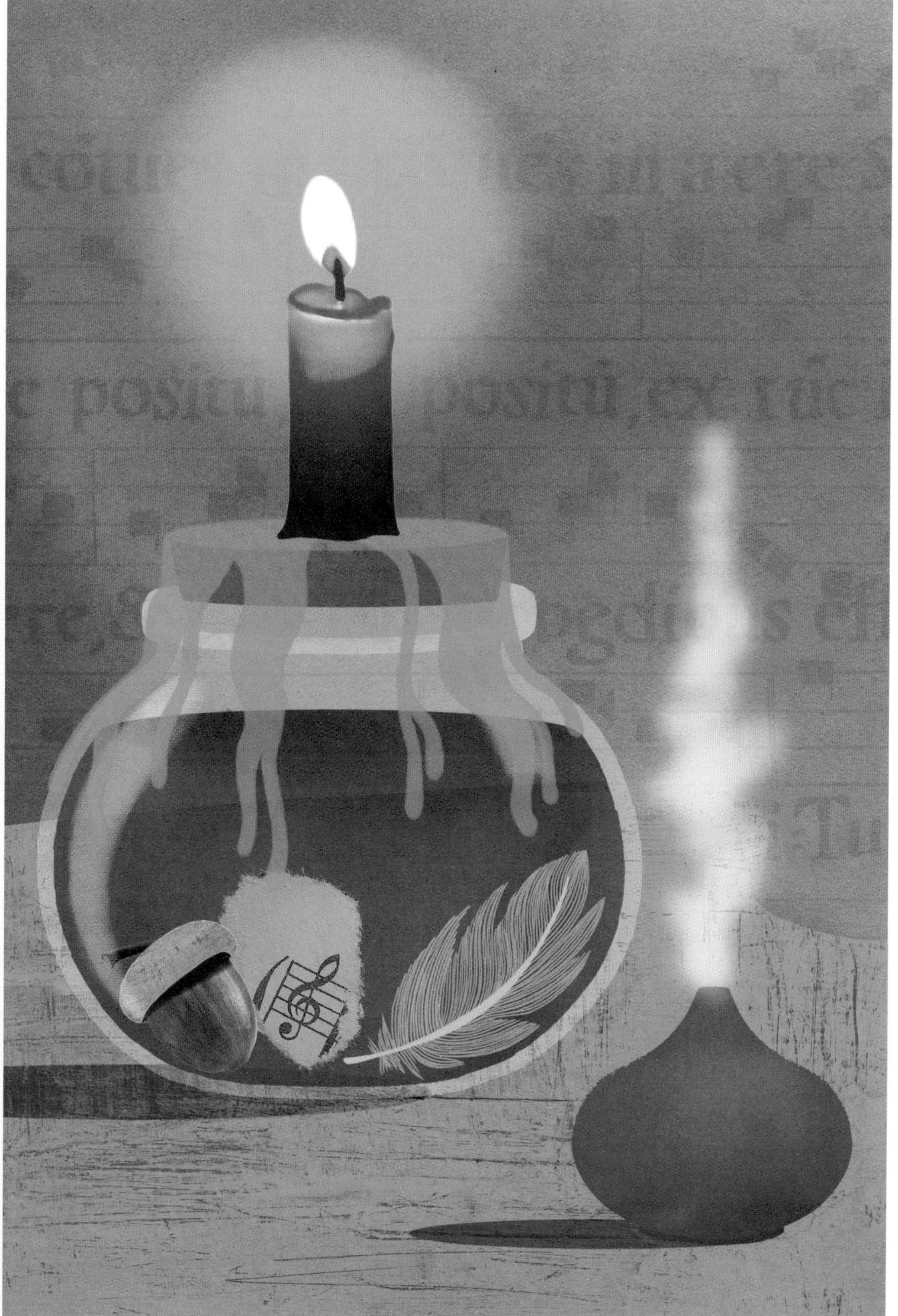

love tisane

Roses and chocolate are classic romantic gifts for a reason—they are the simplest and most straightforward offering of love in a way that cannot be mistaken. Drink this tea to extend that same love to yourself: the love you deserve.

½ teaspoon dried rose petals

½ teaspoon cacao nibs

Honey, to taste

Milk of your choice, to taste

Heat a kettle of water, and let it come to a boil. Turn the heat off and let the water rest for three minutes. While it's resting, add the dried rose petals and cacao nibs to a tea strainer. Slowly pour the water over your strainer, inhaling the steam. Cover your mug with a small plate, and let your tea steep for five minutes. It may need longer, depending on the freshness of your herbs, so test to see if it's ready. If the flavor of the rose and chocolate is present, stir in some honey. Be generous here, for love is sweet. Add some milk, again being generous, for love is comforting.

Inhale deeply before taking your first sip, breathing in the scent of roses and chocolate, luxurious and decadent. As you begin to sip, revel in the sweetness, and remember that love is a gift. It is something we receive with open hands and an open heart—and we give love in the same way. Can you find that openness within yourself, for yourself? Self-love is and must be the place from which all other love grows.

rhubarb lemonade tea

This riff on an Arnold Palmer uses our Love Tisane along with the rhubarb simple syrup, making it simultaneously earthier and more tart than the original. These components add both a grounding, supportive love and a bright, energizing love.

½ cup Love Tisane (see page 52)

Juice of 1 lemon

2 ounces Rhubarb-Infused Simple Syrup (see page 48)

Vodka (optional)

You can make as much tisane as you like, but this recipe calls for only half a cup. Make the tisane as described on page 52, pouring half a cup of just boiled water over your tea strainer of dried rose petals and cacao nibs. Do not cover, but let it cool to room temperature, steeping the whole time. Meanwhile, juice a lemon, and strain out the seeds—you can keep the pulp if you like, for a burst of flavor and texture. Stir the Rhubarb-Infused Simple Syrup into the lemon juice. When your tea has cooled, add the lemon-rhubarb mixture and serve over ice. Spike with vodka if desired, and feel the balance of love within you—both its spark, and its comfort.

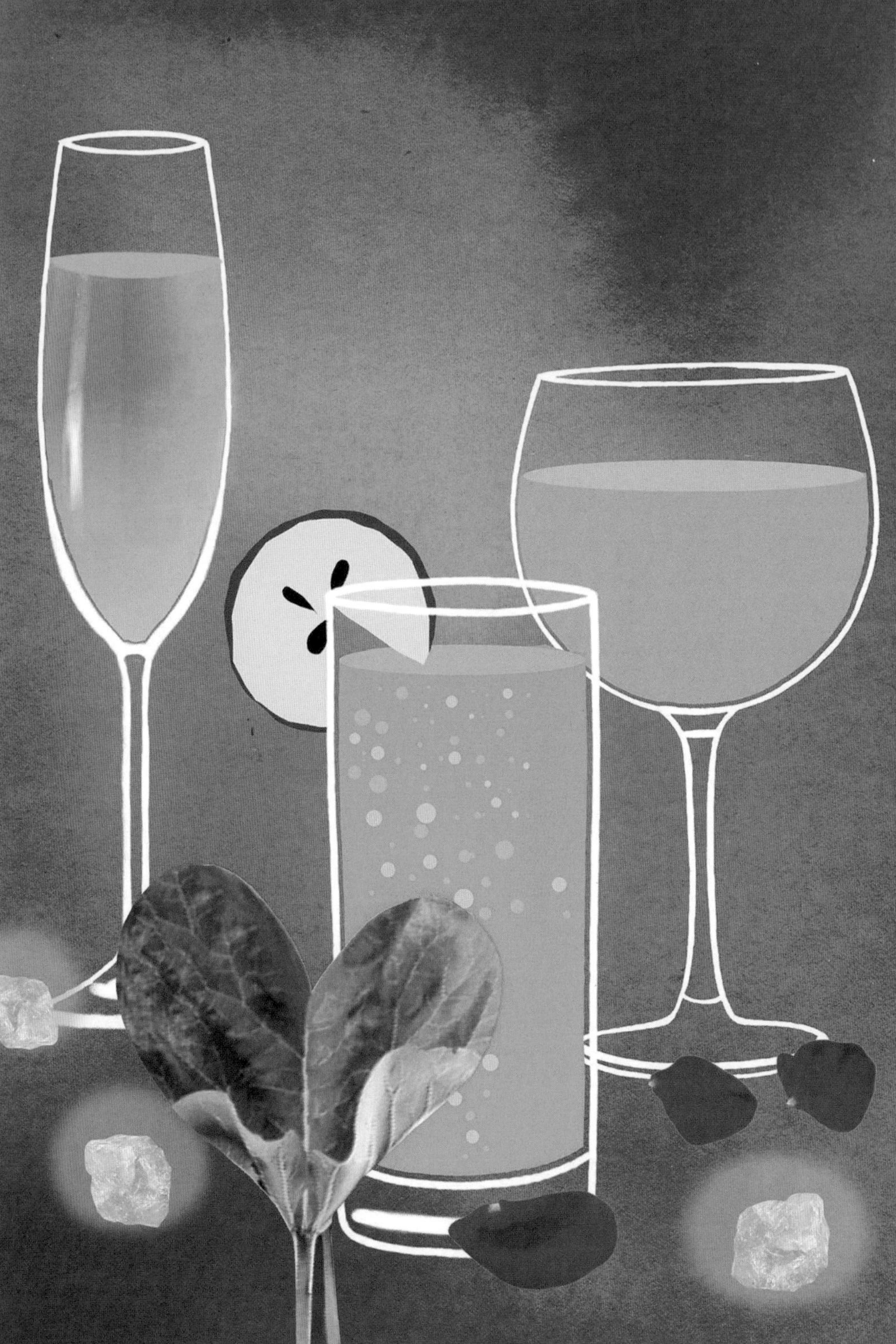

sparkling rhubarb apple

Apples, too, have a long history in love magic. They symbolize connection, fertility, and abundance.

4 ounces natural apple juice

2 teaspoons Rhubarb-Infused Simple Syrup (see page 48)

½ teaspoon Potent Rhubarb Shrub (see page 47)

¼ teaspoon Loving Bitters (see page 46)

Seltzer

Gin (optional)

To a collins glass filled with ice, add the first four ingredients. Top with seltzer and spike with gin if desired. This light, fruity drink hearkens back to celebratory sparkling apple cider that perhaps we would enjoy at holidays when the grown-ups drank wine or champagne. As you sip it, let the magic of your childhood self bubble forth, brimming with joy in simple things.

pink gin

Originating in the mid-1800s, Pink Gin was simply gin flavored with Angostura bitters. The story goes that it was invented by sailors in the British Navy desperate to spike their nausea-preventing bitters with something a little stronger . . . like gin! This variation is sweeter and brighter, and gets is rosy color from rhubarb rather than from bitters. And it is less about prevention than it is an invitation—to see the world in a slightly rosier, more romantic fashion.

2 ounces gin

½ ounce Rhubarb-Infused Simple Syrup (see page 48)

½ teaspoon Potent Rhubarb Shrub (see page 47)

Add all the ingredients to a cocktail shaker and give it a strong shake. Pour into a coupe glass and enjoy, basking in its lovely pink and love-conjuring properties.

mimosa rosé

A mimosa is simply champagne and orange juice, and while sometimes simple things are the best, it's hard not to want to boost the romance and magic of this brunch special. This loving cocktail takes away the orange juice and replaces it with orange-flavored liqueur, and swaps out champagne for delightfully pink sparkling rosé.

1 ounce Witchy Cointreau (see page 24) or store-bought Cointreau

⅛ teaspoon Loving Bitters (see page 46)

Sparkling rosé

Add the Witchy Cointreau and bitters to a champagne glass, then top it off with your chilled sparkling rosé. Toast the people you love with this convivial beverage, particularly the friends closest to your heart—after all, what is a toast but the setting of your intention on goodwill for those honored.

COURAGE

SO MANY THINGS IN LIFE TAKE COURAGE. Sometimes it feels like it takes courage just to get out of bed in the morning and face the new day. Alcohol has long been a potion people have called upon when we don't feel quite up to whatever task is ahead—there's a reason it's called "liquid courage," after all.

The truth, of course, is we have all that we need within us, and no shot of whiskey is going to provide us with abilities we didn't already possess. We call on the aid of potions as a ritual act to dig down deep within to the courage that is already there.

There are so many herbs that can help us find our courage, too. Fennel, mint, ginger, parsley, thyme, and caraway all have strengthening properties. Barley, too, is the source of that liquid courage, so Scotch whiskey is definitely something to be sipped and enjoyed. We can support our potions with crystals like amber, carnelian, garnet, red jasper, agate, bloodstone, and sardonyx.

courageous bitters

Courage doesn't always feel good. It can seem like risk, like the potential for hurt—and it's only on the other side of that risk that we realize when we were brave rather than foolhardy. But that's the thing about courage—we need it when we don't know whether everything will work out. This potion will help you face the unknown.

½ teaspoon fennel seeds

½ teaspoon dried parsley

½ teaspoon dried thyme

½ teaspoon caraway seeds

¼ cup vodka

Combine the herbs and spices in a jar. Cover with a quarter cup of vodka to steep this complex flavor. Put the lid on the jar and shake *hard*—you may even want to jump up and down while you do it! Resist feeling silly if you can, and if you can't, have the courage to do it anyway. As you jump and shake, imagine pouring the energy you want to keep into your tincture, and stomp out all the energy you want to leave behind.

Let your tincture rest in a cool, dark place for two weeks. Place your chosen crystals in a protective circle around it, sealing in its energies. Every few days, visit it for another round of shaking and jumping.

courageous lemon ginger shrub

This shrub follows the basic script for shrubs, with the addition of some ginger and rice vinegar for a slightly sharper flavor. The bold taste and natural heat of ginger will enhance your courage, magically drawing out the strength you hold within.

1 lemon, thinly sliced

½-inch piece of ginger, peeled and thinly sliced

¼ cup sugar

¼ cup rice vinegar

Place the sliced lemon in a jar. Add the peeled and sliced fresh ginger to the lemon. Sprinkle in a quarter cup of sugar and close your jar tightly.

It's time to jump and shake. Put on empowering music if you like—something with a heavy, stomping beat—and rock the heck out of that jar. Shake until your arms hurt and dance until your heart rate has gone up. Be brave.

When you feel complete, choose some courage-building crystals and press them to your solar plexus chakra, invoking your personal power. Then place them in a circle around your jar, sealing in all the energy you conjured up with your shaking. After the lemon and ginger have cured in the sugar for an hour or so, add a quarter cup of rice wine vinegar, then let your shrub steep for three days and three nights. It is ready to decant on the fourth day.

fennel simple syrup and chutney

Fennel is a grounding plant that somehow manages to be both earthy and airy with its sharp anise flavor. In this way, it gives us the firm base we need to jump off from and a bit of ethereal wind at our backs to take flight.

FOR THE SYRUP:
1 fennel bulb

½ cup sugar

FOR THE CHUTNEY:
1 apple

1 tablespoon apple cider vinegar

½ teaspoon salt

¼ teaspoon dried thyme

1 dried red chile

Take a single fennel bulb and chop off the fronds. Peel away the browned and stiff outer layers and discard them, thanking them for keeping the interior of the bulb safe and fresh. Peel the tender layers, roughly chop, and place the pieces in a saucepan. Add the sugar and a half cup of water and bring the mixture to a boil. Let it simmer for 20 minutes or until the fennel is very tender, stirring occasionally in a clockwise motion to invoke the brightness of the sun.

Strain out the fennel, reserving the syrup. If you like, the leftover sweet stewed fennel could be good chopped into a chutney. To make, peel and chop an apple and add it to the saucepan with the reserved stewed fennel. Add the apple cider vinegar, salt, thyme, and dried red chile. Simmer until the liquid is gone and the apples are soft, and adjust seasoning to taste.

ginger kombucha

Ginger Kombucha is probably one of the most popular flavors available. It can calm an upset stomach—a condition that tends to occur if you're feeling less than brave—raise your energy levels, and boost your immune system.

1 batch Basic Kombucha (see page 12)

2-inch piece of fresh ginger, peeled and thinly sliced

At Step 1 of the Basic Kombucha process described on page 13, decant your 7 cups of kombucha into a jar or jars, leaving just a little space at the top of the jar to boost carbonation. Peel the fresh ginger, and thinly slice it, adding the slices to the jar. Inhale their bright, sharp scent, and feel your mind magically clear.

Set your intentions for what you want to brew in this potion. What specifically do you need to be brave for? Is there a challenge headed your way? Focus your attention on meeting that challenge head-on. Seal your jar, and let it steep in your refrigerator for one week. At the end of the week, carefully unscrew it, and take a taste. Does it need to be even stronger? Do you need more powerful carbonation or a sharper flavor? Maybe let this one go just a bit longer, to give it an even stronger punch, then strain out the ginger.

empowering tisane

This tisane uses different spices, but the basic process is inspired by the traditional Ayurvedic masala chai. As such, it brews a lot of tea, much more than a single batch, but you can pop it in the fridge to enjoy as iced or hot tea, as desired; it will keep for a couple of weeks. Each of the herbs and spices here brings a different flavor of courage, with the fennel providing a grounding base, the mint and ginger imparting energy, thyme and caraway offering their innate courage, and parsley giving you its protection.

2 teaspoons whole fennel seeds

2 teaspoons dried mint

1 teaspoon dried thyme

1 teaspoon caraway seeds

1 teaspoon dried parsley

2 inches fresh ginger, peeled and thinly sliced

3 bags green tea

Milk and honey (optional)

Using a mortar and pestle, grind the first five ingredients to a broken gravel. Place the mixture in a pot, and add the remaining ingredients, plus 3 cups of water. Bring to a boil, and then turn off the heat, letting the mixture steep for 10–15 minutes, then strain.

This tea will be spicy and a bit sharp. If you like, you can add milk and honey, as with chai, but consider trying it without. Inhale its bright, spicy fragrance. Take a sip, and hold it in your mouth for a moment (after first checking to make sure it isn't too hot!). Feel its heat fill your mouth, and then swallow it down, sensing the warmth of the tea as it drops down your throat, until it settles comfortably in your belly.

You already have the fire within you. Let the heat of the tea stoke your inner flame, expanding it and bringing it into your awareness.

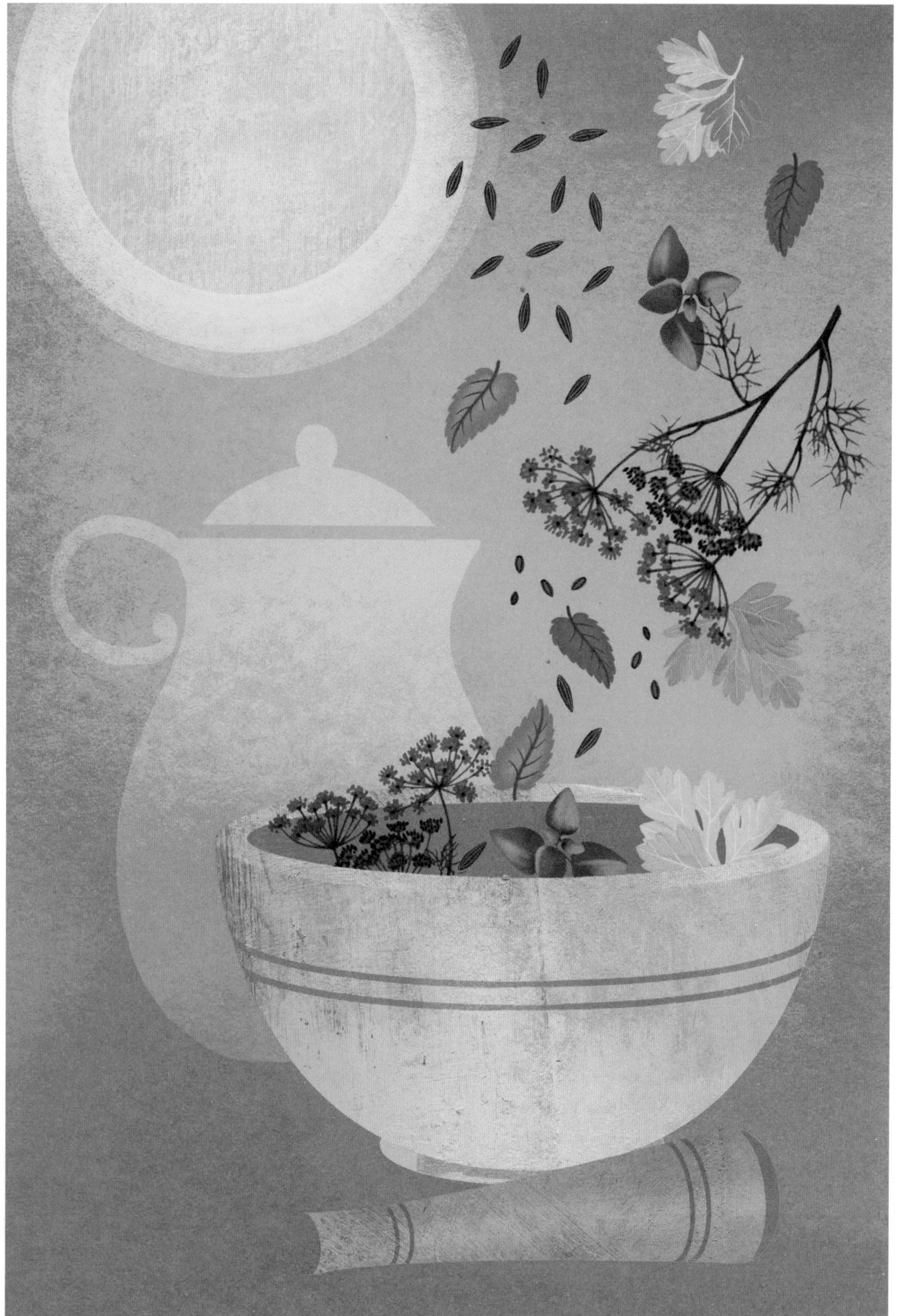

RITUAL FOR COURAGE

There are moments when we just don't have time for an elaborate ritual. When you're just about to head into a meeting to ask for a raise, you don't necessarily have the time—or the privacy—to etch a sigil into a candle or put together a charm bag. But just because a ritual is simple and straightforward doesn't mean it isn't powerful.

Sometimes, we are all we need.

When you want to find that strength within yourself, seek out a quiet space. Close your office door, your bedroom door, or even go outside. All you need is a few moments. Stand with your feet pressed together, your shoulders back, and your arms at your sides. If you practice yoga, you'll recognize this as Mountain Pose or Tadasana.

Close your eyes and imagine that you're standing on a flat pillar in the middle of an ocean. There is no land in sight. The pillar isn't much larger than your feet, which you plant firmly into it. Your chin is lifted, and you don't look down. Waves crash against the pillar, making it rock, but you do not falter. A gust of wind tries to knock you off balance, but it cannot. Breathe deeply, feeling yourself steady and strong, able to withstand all that might try to destabilize you.

When you're ready, open your eyes, and step off of your imaginary pillar. You've got this.

ginger mint limeade

This nonalcoholic riff on a mojito is perfect for a hot, sweaty day, when you may be feeling weighed down by all that is ahead of you. It draws on the invigorating flavors and magic of ginger, mint, and lime to lift you up. Turn to it for a pick-me-up midafternoon, and it will give you the energy and confidence you need to not only get through the day, but thrive in it.

¾ cup lime juice, from approximately 6 limes

1½ cups Simple Syrup (see page 10)

½-inch piece of ginger

2 tablespoons mint leaves, whole

A sprig of mint

Light rum (optional)

Juice approximately six limes, or enough to get you the right amount of liquid. Stir in 4 cups of water and the Simple Syrup. Chill this base limeade while you prepare your other ingredients.

Peel the fresh ginger and mash it in a mortar and pestle to release its juices. Add the mint leaves to your mortar and pestle, and bruise them with the ginger. Add the ginger and mint to your limeade and stir well. Serve over ice with a sprig of mint, and add a dash of light rum to spike, as desired.

fizzy fennel

This refreshingly earthy drink takes the anise flavor of fennel and lets it sit brightly and sweetly on the tongue. It will calm the nerves and ground you, keeping you focused in the present and certain of your own truth, whatever your fears may be.

1–2 ounces Fennel Simple Syrup (see page 62)

2 dashes (¼ teaspoon) Courageous Bitters (see page 60)

Sparkling water

Lemon wedge

Fennel frond

Dry white wine (optional)

Add the Fennel Simple Syrup to a collins glass filled with ice. Add the Courageous Bitters, and top with sparkling water, adding more syrup to taste. Add a squeeze of lemon and garnish with a fennel frond. Spike with a dry white wine if desired.

gin sling

Apparently, when the sling was first invented before Prohibition, it was meant to be tossed back (i.e., "slung"), like a shot. But of course, in those days, it was a much simpler drink—just a bit of sugar dissolved in some gin with a dash of nutmeg. Needless to say, it has improved and is worth sipping rather than throwing into your throat. This variation on a classic gin sling includes Courageous Bitters rather than the typical Angostura, and it can give you the heady, dancing energy you need to overcome any fears.

1½ ounces gin

1 ounce sweet vermouth

¾ ounce fresh lemon juice

¾ ounce Simple Syrup (see page 10)

⅛ teaspoon Courageous Bitters (see page 60)

2 ounces seltzer

Twist of lemon

Add the first six ingredients to a rocks glass and stir well. Add ice and garnish with a twist of lemon. Sip, don't sling.

penicillin

A traditional Penicillin contains Scotch, honey, ginger syrup, and lemon juice. The theory is that whatever bug you've got, this drink will knock it out of you. Well, in a slightly healthier approach, this version of a Penicillin uses your Ginger Kombucha. You want a good, peaty Scotch for this—even if it isn't ordinarily to your taste, that funky, smoky flavor will give you the kick in the pants you need to get up and face whatever it is that's been bugging you. Is there a habit you want to get rid of or a difficult conversation you've been stewing over? This potion combines the wisdom of age found in Scotch with the fresh, new life of kombucha to give you the fortitude you need.

2 ounces Scotch

Ginger Kombucha (see page 63)

Lemon wedge

Pour out the smoky Scotch (like Laphroaig, Talisker, or Lagavulin) into a collins glass filled with ice. Top with Ginger Kombucha, and add a squeeze of lemon. Sip that liquid courage.

BALANCE

IT'S A TRICKY CONCEPT, BALANCE. HOW DO we know when we've achieved it? How do we know we're paying enough attention to our families and friends? Whether we're working hard enough at our jobs, or perhaps too hard? Whether we're doing enough self-care? How can we ever be sure we're considering all of that at the same time, to the same extent?

The truth is, we can't. Sometimes a friend will be in crisis and you'll come running, but next month she will be there to support you. Sometimes you have a deadline at work and have to skip yoga class, but perhaps you can go on retreat at your next hard-earned vacation. It's not about everything being level from moment to moment, but seeking equilibrium over the long term—and like enlightenment, it is something you will *always* be seeking.

Finding balance requires paying attention. It calls for listening to yourself, and to others, and leaning in when you can and pulling back when you have to. We are supported in this constant motion by a variety of herbs and crystals. Lavender, mint, mullein, lemon, coconut, and barley can all help us maintain our balance, as can clear quartz, moonstone, pearl, sunstone, tigereye, and yellow jasper.

balancing bitters

Mullein is also known as "torch plant." Before cotton became popular for this use, dried mullein was used as a wick for oil lanterns, and the seed heads soaked in oil can serve as a kind of tiki torch. Consider it a guiding light, keeping you on a balanced path.

Peel of 1 lemon

1 teaspoon dried mullein

¼ cup vodka

Peel a lemon with your vegetable peeler, and pop the peels on a baking sheet to roast at 200°F for an hour. When they're done, allow them to cool, then place them in a jar and add the dried mullein. Cover with a quarter cup of vodka and shut tightly. Let your tincture sit in a cool, dark place for two weeks, surrounded by your chosen crystals for balance (see pages 5–6). Every few days, tip it back and forth, angling your wrist so it turns upside down and then right side up. This is what life does to us, flipping us over and over. It's all right. Sometimes it's even beneficial.

balancing lemon mint shrub

In magic, as in life, we are always seeking balance. Think of how we ask our Mother Earth for aid and strength, as we also seek to honor and give back to her. Or how we work to maintain a sense of harmony between all of our chakras. This shrub takes that same idea, bringing balance to your potion and infusing that into your future concoctions.

1 lemon, thinly sliced

¼ cup sugar

¼ cup white wine vinegar

A sprig of mint

Thinly slice a lemon. Add the slices to a jar, and sprinkle in the quarter cup of sugar. Close the jar tightly and shake it upside down and right side up, over and over, so that each lemon slice is coated. Place the jar on the counter, and surround it with balancing crystals. If you like, place your crystals in a line, with the jar at the center, as if the jar is a fulcrum. Let your crystals infuse the lemons with their energy for an hour, then add the quarter cup of white wine vinegar and sprig of mint. Let this sit for three days and three nights. Give it a shake at least once a day, turning it upside down and right side up. On the morning of the fourth day, strain out the liquid.

lemon-infused rum

In this potion, we are giving a hint of the tartness of lemon to the sweet palate of rum. As with all alcoholic infusions, you don't need to use the best of the best, but you will want a white or clear rum like Bacardi or Captain Morgan—and make sure it is unflavored.

6 lemons, thinly sliced

4 cups white or clear rum

Thinly slice the lemons and place them in a large jar. Add the rum, and store in a cool, dry place. Place a balancing crystal nearby to help bind together the two flavors. Let your infusion rest for three to seven days, giving it a taste every now and then to make sure it's achieved the balance of flavors you desire—and the balance of the sweet relaxation of rum with the energetic brightness lemon, finding that fulcrum in between, where you can be both vibrant and calm. Strain out the lemons and store in a cool, dry place.

lemon mint kombucha

If achieving balance requires paying attention, this bright kombucha will help you find clarity as you sip it with intent, so that you aren't overwhelmed by the many demands on your time and energy.

1 batch Basic Kombucha (see page 12)

2 lemons, thinly sliced

Handful of mint leaves, roughly chopped

At Step 1 of the Basic Kombucha process described on page 13, decant 7 cups of kombucha into a jar or jars, leaving a little room at the top. Slice two lemons thinly and add them to the jar. Roughly chop a handful of mint leaves, inhaling their refreshing scent, and add them to the jar, as well. Seal the jar well, and gently turn it upside down and right side up a few times. Balance isn't something we have every single day, it's something we experience over time. Let this potion brew for a week, as it imbues itself with the clarity that will be passed on to you.

balancing tisane

Magic is all about intention—and intention requires us to ask questions and tune in deeply to our thoughts and feelings. Through both the ingredients and brewing process of this tisane, learn to listen to yourself, as you restore balance to this moment.

½ teaspoon lavender

½ teaspoon dried mint

¼ teaspoon mullein

Squeeze of lemon

Spoonful of honey, to taste

Bring some water to a boil, then turn it off and let it come to stillness, all that activity finding rest. In a tea strainer, combine the lavender, mint, and mullein. Pour the water over the strainer and into your cup, letting it steep for three minutes. Remove the strainer and add a squeeze of lemon and a spoonful of honey, stirring to mix everything. Take a first sip of your tisane, and ask yourself what is most needed at this moment. Should you find some time to do something that brings you pleasure? Should you go through your email? Should you call a friend? The correct answer will change from day to day, so whenever you prepare this potion for yourself, allow the response to float up with the steam.

BALANCING RITUAL

Balance is something we have to tend to—it's something that requires and deserves our attention. But how do we know if we are doing that adequately? One way to test our emotional and spiritual balance is to practice physical balance, embodying that state of leaning first this way and then that to find the upright center.

Come into Tree Pose, or Vrksasana. Begin by standing with your feet together, then lift one leg. Place your foot firmly against the inside of the standing leg, either above or below the knee, whichever is more comfortable. Let your hands rest at your sides, at your waist, or if you like, reach them high above your head.

Are you wobbling a little? Does your standing foot rock back and forth, your toes gripping the floor beneath you? Is your other foot sliding toward the earth? Are you tilting one way or the other? Do you fall out of the pose?

These are all normal responses to being thrown off balance. It's natural. Come out of the pose for a moment and take a deep breath. Close your eyes. What are you feeling, inside? What seems out of balance, as if one leg has been pulled out from under you?

Come into Mountain Pose (see page 66). Lift your heart and let your shoulders relax. Engage your core—the muscles of your abdomen—and now lift the opposite leg into Tree Pose. Find a spot on the wall or the floor in front of you to focus on, letting everything else in your line of sight blur and drift away. Pay attention to that spot, and also to the sensation of your foot pressing against the floor, and your other foot pressing against your leg. If you begin to rock, use your core to keep yourself upright.

It still isn't easy, keeping our balance, but it's *easier* if we pay attention and use the tools and skills we have to maintain our equilibrium, even when circumstances make it difficult. These same skills—lifting your heart, focusing inward, and using the strength within—will always help you find your balance again, even if you've fallen down.

pursuit of balance

The refreshing and grounding properties of coconut water shine in this balance of sweet, bitter, and tart.

½ ounce Balancing Lemon Mint Shrub (see page 75)

2 dashes (¼ teaspoon) Balancing Bitters (see page 74)

Handful of mint leaves

Coconut water

A sprig of mint

Lemon-Infused Rum (see page 77) (optional)

Add the first three ingredients to a collins glass, and muddle them together. Add ice and fill with coconut water. Garnish with a sprig of mint, and spike with Lemon-Infused Rum, as desired. Consider this drink like a vacation, a trip to a tropical island that refreshes, reinvigorates, and restores. We all need a break now and then.

transportive piña colada

Continuing along the vacation theme, sometimes you just need a treat. That's all the balance that's required—something sweet and refreshing that makes you feel like you're relaxing on a beach somewhere even in the midst of a snowstorm. That, after all, is the power of magic—to invoke within ourselves a transportive idea that transcends our present circumstances and conjures forth that which we need in the moment.

3 cups frozen pineapple chunks

1 can full-fat coconut milk

1–2 ounces Simple Syrup (see page 10)

Rum (optional)

Fill a blender with frozen pineapple chunks and a can of coconut milk—full fat, because remember, this is a treat! Add the Simple Syrup to taste, and blend the whole thing on high until smooth. Garnish with a straw umbrella, and add rum, as desired, for an instant beach in a glass.

balanced on a volcano

This drink is a somewhat distanced riff on a traditional Malcolm Lowry (named after the author of Under the Volcano*), which calls for lime juice and tequila. This admittedly unusual shift to pairing lemon with mezcal results in a drink that feels like a more surprising margarita. It's bright, tangy, bitter, smoky, salty,* and *sweet—and somehow all the flavors blend together, balancing each other out.*

Mezcal can be a bit of an acquired taste, as its flavor is earthy and strong. According to legend, mezcal was "discovered" when lightning struck an agave plant, splitting open its core—and this beverage poured forth from its heart. It gives a sense of clarity and openness, partially due to its low sugar content. As mezcal is usually brewed in small batches, it also contains fewer additives and is often organic.

2 ounces fresh-squeezed lemon juice

Salt

1 ounce mezcal

¾ ounce Lemon-Infused Rum (see page 77)

½ ounce Witchy Cointreau (see page 24) or triple sec

After juicing your lemons, use the leftover lemon halves to moisten the rim of a coupe glass. Dip the glass in a plate of salt, tapping off any excess. Fill a shaker with ice and add the mezcal, Lemon-Infused Rum, Witchy Cointreau, and lemon juice, along with a small pinch of salt. Shake well, flipping the shaker end over end at least once, then strain into the glass. Allow yourself to be fully present in the moment as you take a sip, experiencing the symphony of balance that arises out of these seemingly disparate ingredients. How can you bring that poise into your own life and practice?

balancing boulevardier

This drink is not quite a vacation, but rather a return to the more challenging parts of life—for we cannot escape them entirely, nor should we. A Boulevardier is a variation on a Negroni, using whiskey instead of gin. It's complex and a little bitter, something to be sipped and enjoyed slowly with thoughtful attention. As you drink, ask yourself: What have you been neglecting?

While this recipe calls for rye whiskey, you can also use bourbon if you like something a little sweeter. Both rye and bourbon almost always contain some amount of barley grain, which will help to boost this potion's balancing qualities.

1 ounce rye whiskey

1 ounce sweet vermouth

1 ounce Campari

Twist of lemon

Fill a rocks glass with ice and add the first three ingredients. Garnish with a twist of lemon, and let it sit for a minute or two before serving, so that the spirits have time to chili and blend.

HARMONY

ATTAINING HARMONY REQUIRES A RESONANCE with something external, whether that is nature, your partner, family, coworkers, or even the world in general. We often feel a bit off-key, as if we are simply not connecting with those around us. We aren't in flow.

When this happens, it is easy to wish that the world would align with *us*, rather than the other way around. Why does everyone else have it so wrong? But the truth is that harmony doesn't actually mean being fully in alignment—we don't have to *feel* the same way as everyone else or *agree* with them. All harmony requires is a sympathetic point of view, a way of singing our own tune—not anyone else's—but somehow that allows other sounds to come through pleasantly and not as a cacophony of warring notes.

It isn't easy. It requires listening and making minute adjustments. But it's worth it, because it's how we can make sure our voice is heard, and not lost in the noise. Basil, mint, elderflower, lemon balm, strawberry, potatoes, and clove can all support us in finding harmony, as can carnelian, malachite, and clear quartz.

bitters for harmony

The anise scent and flavor of basil find a balance between the brightness of orange and the grounded spice of cloves. These magical herbs come together to form a chorus in this potion.

1 orange

½ teaspoon dried basil

½ teaspoon cloves

¼ cup vodka

Peel half the orange with your vegetable peeler, and place the peels on a baking sheet. Roast at 200°F for an hour, then allow to cool. Place the dried peels in a jar and add the dried basil and cloves. Cover with a quarter cup of vodka and close the jar tightly. Rest your tincture in a cool, dark place for two weeks, surrounded by your chosen crystals for harmony (see pages 5–6). Every day or two, give it a gentle shake, and see if you can find a rhythm. You might even hum a favorite tune—just for a few moments—singing to your tincture and letting it hear and integrate your own distinctive voice.

basil lemon shrub for harmony

Basil comes in to sing the melody in this potion, with lemon providing backup. Basil nourishes the energies powered by the chakras, working to bring each of them into alignment with one another.

1 lemon, thinly sliced

¼ cup sugar

¼ cup white wine vinegar

Handful of fresh basil leaves

Thinly slice the lemon, and place the slices in a jar. Sprinkle in a quarter cup of sugar, and then close the jar tightly. Give it a rhythmic shake, and again consider singing to it! Just for a moment or two—even if it feels silly. When the lemon slices are fully coated, let the jar rest on the counter for an hour, then add the white wine vinegar and handful of fresh basil leaves. Place your crystals for harmony nearby, and let your shrub infuse for three days and three nights. Sing to it and shake it now and again, just in passing. On the morning of the fourth day, strain out the liquid.

strawberry-infused vodka

Strawberries are the only fruit with seeds on the exterior. In this way, they are vulnerable and trusting, putting their most treasured assets on display for all to see. They live in faith that their trust will be repaid. This is harmony in nature, and this potion infuses the blank slate of vodka with the essence of strawberry.

2 cups strawberries, thinly sliced

4 cups vodka

Wash your strawberries, then slice them thinly. Add the sliced strawberries to a large jar, then cover with the vodka. Store in a cool, dry place, surrounded by crystals for harmony—you might consider carnelian for the strawberries and clear quartz for the vodka to draw on the color correspondence.

Let your potion steep for three to seven days. It's ready when the strawberry flavor is pronounced and on display—and will be there to help boost your inner song.

strawberry basil kombucha

The sweet tang of strawberries combines with the anise freshness of basil to form a harmonious whole. Strawberries grow in a sprawl, feeling their way across the ground and sometimes even up steep inclines to seek fertile ground. Their seeds can sprout even in the harshest of conditions, finding their way to the light. This potion will inspire you to follow their example whether you sip it on its own or combine it in the recipes to come.

1 batch Basic Kombucha (see page 12)

2 cups strawberries, thinly sliced

Handful of basil, torn

At Step 1 of the Basic Kombucha process described on page 13, decant 7 cups of kombucha into a jar or jars, leaving some room at the top. Thinly slice the strawberries and place them in the jar. Tear a handful of basil, releasing its scent and juices, and add this to the jar. Seal the jar well, and shake it gently. Give it just a bit more of your song, and then let your potion steep for a week, letting it settle as the flavors develop and ferment into a bright sparkle.

mint tisane

Sometimes the simplest things can help the most. A cup of mint tea calls us back to childhood—to chewing on mint leaves plucked from the ground. If you're feeling anxious, mint tea can slow your nervous system, and it can also calm an upset stomach. It's caffeine-free, but it still provides a little energy boost. While you can certainly use dried mint or store-bought tea bags, consider getting a small bouquet of fresh mint at the store or from your garden.

Small bunch of fresh leaves or 4 teaspoons dried mint

Sugar, to taste

Lemon juice, to taste

Wash your bouquet of mint well, pluck the leaves, and place them in a teapot. If you have a clear glass jug, consider using it here, so you can see the mint leaves as they steep and unfurl, miraculously retaining their green hue. Pour 2 cups of just-boiled water over your leaves, and allow your tisane to steep for at least five minutes, to get a strong flavor. Stir in some sugar, if you like, or some lemon—or both! You can also allow the tea to come to room temperature, and serve it over ice.

Share your tisane with someone. It doesn't have to be someone you've been struggling to connect with—although if that is the case, mint will help improve your communication. But don't worry about working at it; simply enjoy your tea and enjoy each other's company. Sometimes that's all that's needed.

RITUAL FOR HARMONY

We carry energy centers within us—you have probably heard them called *chakras*, an idea derived from Hindu and Buddhist traditions. In order for us to be at ease with ourselves and others, each of these chakras must resonate together. There are seven of them, which makes for a complex chorus of sound, but then again, we are complex beings. We have to maintain harmony every day, with far more than seven different perspectives and energies. It is a challenge, but we can make it easier by finding harmony within.

To bring your chakras into balance, find a seat on the ground, so that your root chakra is connected with the earth. Sit as straight as you can, aligning each of the chakras with one another so that they stretch in a dotted line up to the sky. If you like, hold a clear quartz crystal in your nondominant hand, with your palm open and faceup.

Now put your attention on each of the seven chakras, working your way from bottom to top:

ROOT CHAKRA. Muladhara, your place of safety. Your connection with ancestors, and with the past. Visualize its swirling red energy, seated right at the base of the spine. Inhale deeply and exhale with a chanted LAM.

SACRAL CHAKRA. Svadisthana, the source of your creativity and sexuality. This is where you find pleasure, both physically and spiritually. Imagine it as an orange swirl in your lower belly. Inhale deeply and exhale as you chant VAM.

SOLAR PLEXUS CHAKRA. Manipura, your power source. This is where you can reach for your inner strength, your resources. You have all that you need within you. Visualize its swirling yellow energy in your core. Inhale deeply and exhale as you chant RAM.

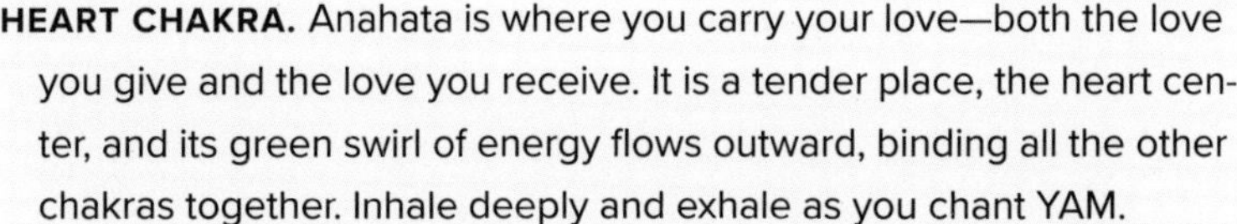

HEART CHAKRA. Anahata is where you carry your love—both the love you give and the love you receive. It is a tender place, the heart center, and its green swirl of energy flows outward, binding all the other chakras together. Inhale deeply and exhale as you chant YAM.

THROAT CHAKRA. Visuddha is a light blue swirl located right at the base of your throat. It is the source of your voice, your true self that you can share with the world, as you live authentically and in alignment with what is right for *you*. Inhale deeply and exhale as you chant HAM.

THIRD EYE CHAKRA. Ajna is located right between the brows, an indigo swirl that lights up your vision, allowing you to see clearly. This is your connection to your intuition, to what is true no matter what feels "logical." Inhale deeply and exhale as you chant OHM.

CROWN CHAKRA. This final chakra, Sahasrara, is located just above the top of your head, outside of your physical body. It is your connection with the realm outside of the physical, whether you call that Source or God or the Universe. Inhale deeply and exhale as you chant OHM.

Having now activated each of your chakras, take a moment to feel them one by one, swirling and moving with their own individual signatures. Then, continuing to breathe deeply, imagine them blending together, the tendrils of their swirls combining like galaxies within you. As each melds into the next, their individual colors become a blurred rainbow, creating one single source of energy. Continue to bring them into resonance with one another, until at last they become a harmonious whole, as your body shines with white light. This is you, integrated and complete.

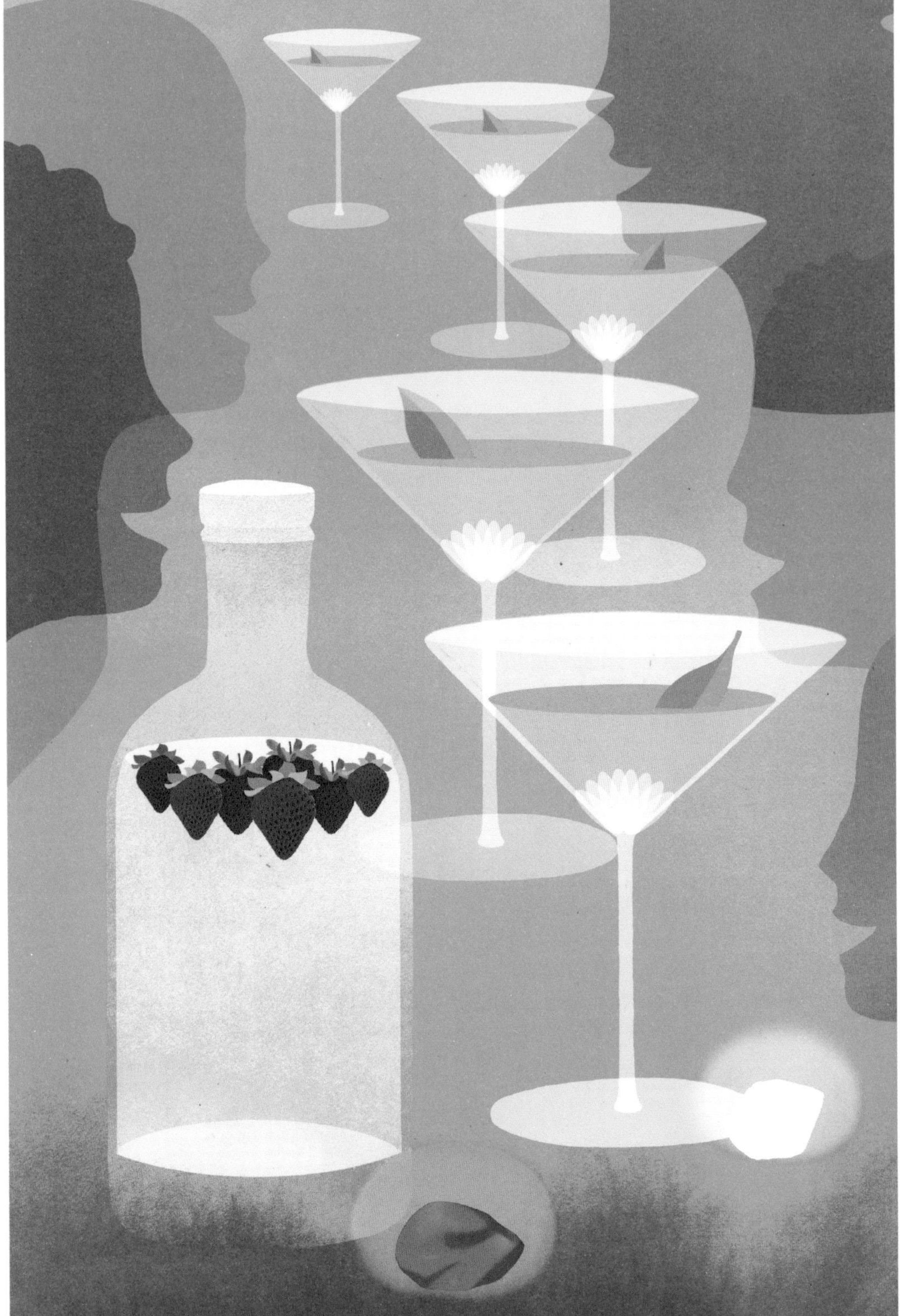

herbs for harmony

This cocktail takes advantage of a chorus of herbs to flavor our Strawberry-Infused Vodka. The result is a delicate but balanced potion that is meant to be sipped slowly and lightly, savored while enjoying a conversation with friends and invoking the magic that happens when we take the time and space to revel in each other's company.

¼ teaspoon Bitters for Harmony (see page 88)

Small handful of basil leaves, torn

½ ounce lemon juice

2 ounces Strawberry-Infused Vodka (see page 90)

½ ounce St. Germain elderflower liqueur

Basil leaf

Muddle the first three ingredients at the bottom of a shaker. Add ice, the vodka, and the St. Germain, then shake well. Strain into a martini glass and garnish with a basil leaf.

harmonious strawberries

This boisson lies somewhere between a smoothie and a juice, with enough texture to keep things interesting without requiring a blender and serving as a full meal. Sip it slowly, intentionally, drawing on the mystical harmony of strawberries to bring alignment to your own world.

2–4 fresh strawberries, cored

1–2 ounces Simple Syrup (see page 10), to taste

Small handful of fresh basil, torn

Strawberry Basil Kombucha (see page 91)

Vodka or Strawberry-Infused Vodka (see page 90) (optional)

Add your strawberries, Simple Syrup, and basil to the bottom of a collins glass. Muddle them together, squashing the strawberries and breaking them down, letting them meld into a harmonious whole, rather than separate pieces. Add ice and fill with kombucha. Give it all a good stir, and spike it with vodka or even Strawberry-Infused Vodka if you really want to go crazy with the strawberries.

synchronous strawberry daiquiri

There is nothing better than a frozen strawberry daiquiri, and honestly, you don't even need the rum—the flavor is there regardless, and it's just as refreshing and feels like just as much of a treat. When we freeze our strawberries—or any plant, for that matter—we are holding them in stasis, capturing them in time. The strawberries we buy from the freezers at the grocery store are flash-frozen at the height of freshness, arresting that moment. Of course, actual *fresh strawberries are even better, but there's a lesson to be learned, a message to be heard, from the freezing of time—a note held, a moment drawn out. As you sip this potion, take the time to appreciate the harmony of life around. Let each moment stretch out, and feel gratitude for the time and space we have.*

1 cup frozen strawberries

1 ounce Simple Syrup (see page 10)

1 ounce lime juice

½ cup Strawberry Basil Kombucha (see page 91)

Sliced strawberry, for garnish

Rum (optional)

Place all the ingredients but the garnish into a blender and run on high until smooth. Pour into a collins glass and garnish with a sliced fresh strawberry. And of course, spike with rum as desired! Sip on a hot day or after a workout, when your body has been stressed and feels out of sync. Let this drink bring your body back into peace, at harmony with the world.

sukha whiskey sour

A sour cocktail is defined as anything that has a balance of sweetness and tartness, blending the three flavors—citrus, sugar, and the liquor—until they reach a harmonious state. They are considered somewhat "accessible" cocktails; sours are easy drinking, if you will. Not only is there nothing wrong with that—after all, shouldn't we want *to enjoy our potions?—there is something inspiring about that ease, that balance. In yoga, we strive to find the* sukha*, the ease within a challenging pose, and this potion is about finding the ease in our daily lives.*

You can use just about anything you like to create a sour, but sometimes, the classics are the best. (Some sours include an egg white, but unless you're using eggs from the chickens next door, there's some risk involved there.) This sour uses bourbon, a sweeter corn-based whiskey that allows all three flavors to shine through equally, like a major chord.

2 ounces bourbon

¾ ounce fresh-squeezed lemon juice

¾ ounce Simple Syrup (see page 10)

Add all the ingredients to an ice-filled shaker. Shake very hard, putting some muscle into it, while slowly counting to 10. Strain into a coupe glass and serve straight up.

PROTECTION

PROTECTION IS ALWAYS AN ESSENTIAL PART of any witch's practice. We are always under attack, it seems—by everyday stressors, violence in the news, health crises, financial worries, and concerns for our loved ones. And that's not even considering the psychic energy we carry—which doesn't even necessarily belong to us! Think about how even an insignificant encounter can shift your energy. Say you've been cut off in traffic or bumped into on the train. It was unpleasant and it wasn't your fault, but it's put you in a bad mood. In all likelihood, that person was probably in a bad mood from something in their life—a challenge at work, an argument at home—and their mood got transferred to you.

For better or worse, interactions with other people will always have an impact on us, but we can mitigate that influence by protecting ourselves and shielding our psychic energy. There are a lot of resources for magical support in nature, including parsley, yarrow, pine, potato, juniper, pepper, blackberry, and raspberry. For crystalline assistance, we can turn to hematite, smoky quartz, obsidian, black tourmaline, and pyrite.

bitters for protection

These bitters have a very distinct flavor, making them a little less versatile than others, but they certainly pack a punch. It's important to source your ingredients carefully; while all pine species are edible, not all evergreens are, so you want to make sure you're using pine. If you're foraging, choose younger needles as they'll be less brittle and have a lighter flavor. You can also find pine needle tea at most natural food stores.

1 teaspoon dried pine needles

1 teaspoon dried yarrow

¼ cup vodka

If you're using fresh pine needles, gather a half cup's worth, then roast them at 200°F for an hour before beginning your potion. Place the dried needles—either dried in an oven or from a tea—in a jar, and add the dried yarrow. Cover with a quarter cup of vodka and close the jar tightly. Rest your tincture in a cool, dark place for two weeks, surrounded by your chosen crystals for protection (see pages 5–6). Every day or two, give it a gentle shake. Visualize a barrier surrounding your tincture, safeguarding it as it will safeguard you.

protective lemon parsley shrub

Parsley is an intriguing herb; the ancient Romans believed that it provided strength and conferred great power. But European folklore held that, due to its long germination period, parsley was connected with death and rebirth, like the myth of Persephone. We can think of it as conferring both types of energy—giving you strength when you need it, but also sheltering you during times of rest and rejuvenation.

1 lemon, thinly sliced

¼ cup sugar

¼ cup white wine vinegar

A sprig of parsley

Slice the lemon thinly, then place the slices in a jar. Sprinkle the quarter cup of sugar over it, then close the jar and shake it, coating each lemon slice with sugar.

Set the jar to rest on a counter. Choose crystals to surround it for protection. You might press each crystal to your root chakra, helping you to feel safer and more grounded, and then to your solar plexus chakra, so that you know you have the power to protect yourself, before you set them around the jar. Let your crystals infuse the lemons with their protective energy for an hour, then add the quarter cup of white wine vinegar and sprig of parsley. Let this sit for three days and three nights. Give it a shake from time to time, protecting its development as it will protect you.

On the morning of the fourth day, strain out the liquid. It's ready for you.

raspberry blackberry kombucha

The raspberry and blackberry in this kombucha form a delicious but powerful barrier between you and anything that may want to invade your space, whether that's a virus—since they're high in vitamin C—or negative energy. You can think of this like a potion version of the thorny hedge surrounding Sleeping Beauty's castle.

1 batch Basic Kombucha (see page 12)

¼ cup raspberries (fresh or frozen)

¼ cup blackberries (fresh or frozen)

1 bunch of parsley, roughly chopped

At Step 1 of the Basic Kombucha process described on page 13, decant 7 cups of kombucha into a jar or jars, leaving some room at the top. Add the raspberries, the blackberries, and the bunch of parsley. Seal the jar well, and shake it gently. Let your potion steep in the refrigerator for one week, fermenting and developing its flavor and protective qualities.

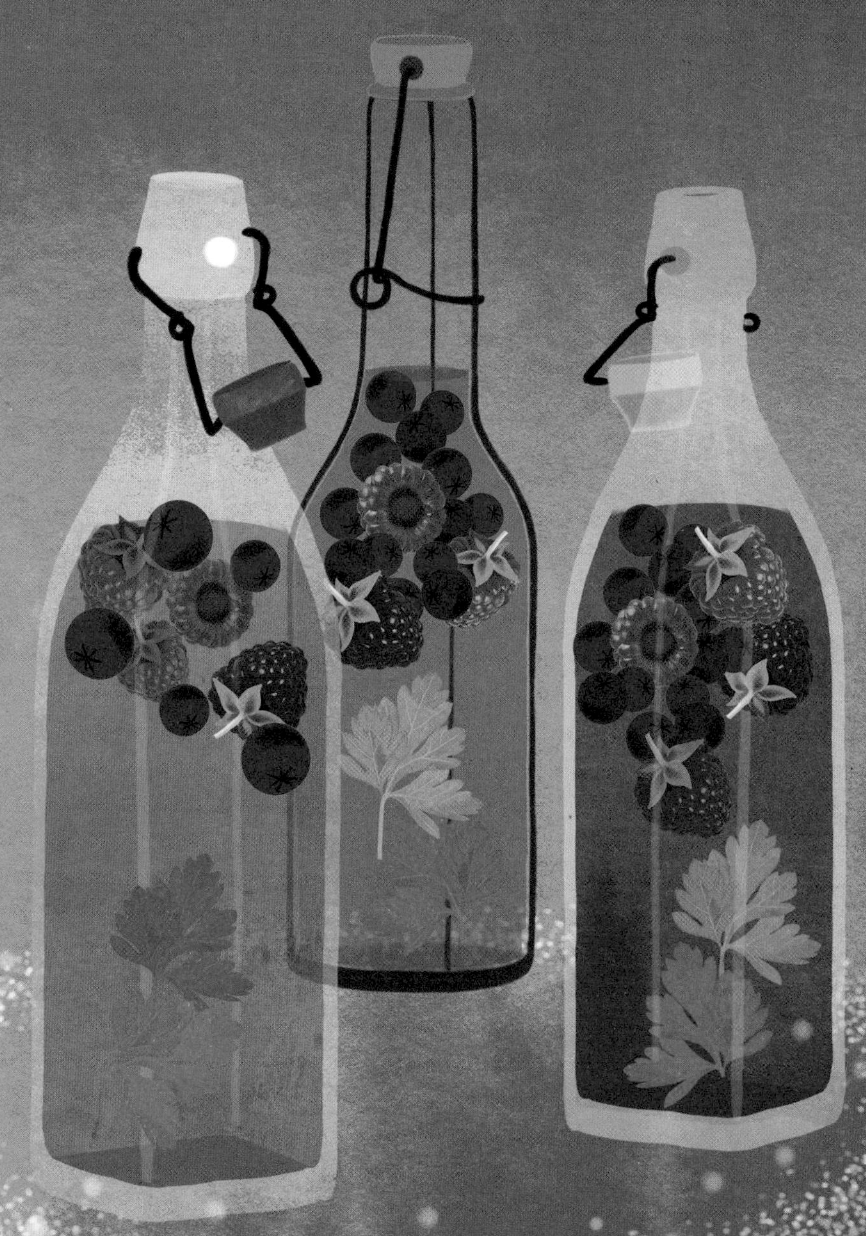

pepper-infused vodka

Pepper-infused vodka is more versatile than you'd think—you can serve it with some muddled raspberries topped with soda (similar to page 111), you can mix it with ginger beer and lime for a spicy vodka mule, or you can go the more obvious (and beloved) route and make a Bloody Mary, as on page 115. This potion gives a jolt of flavor—enough that you'll know *its protective magic is working.*

2 tablespoons peppercorns

4 cups vodka

Put the peppercorns in a jar and cover with the vodka. Let your infusion rest, nestled with hematite or black tourmaline, in a cool, dry place for a maximum of four days—more than that, and your infusion may be *too* spicy.

protective tisane

Fair warning, the flavors of this tea are a little on the sharp side. After all, it is acting as a psychic barrier, so it makes sense that it tastes a little thorny.

1 teaspoon dried mixed parsley, pine, yarrow, raspberry leaf

Combine the dried herbs for a total of 1 teaspoon. Put your mixture in a tea strainer, and shake it up a bit to distribute them evenly. Pour some just-boiled water over the strainer, and as you allow your tisane to steep, visualize a barrier surrounding it, much like the wall of thorns around Sleeping Beauty. Within this barricade you don't need to be rescued from anything; instead, you need to be allowed to enjoy your peace and space.

After five minutes, take your tea to your favorite chair or somewhere you feel safe and comfortable. As you sip, imagine that thorny barrier expanding over you, surrounding you. Nothing can get in—unless you allow it.

PROTECTION RITUAL

We all need to have a place where we feel secure, that proverbial tower where nothing can get us. It's high up and there's no door, and that thorny hedge is there for good measure. Of course, such a physical refuge doesn't exist, and without it sometimes it can be hard not to think that Rapunzel had it pretty good.

But when we're *not* feeling stressed and unsafe, we know that living tucked away from the world would be akin to a prison. The key is to have, well, a key—a way to block negative energy, but let in positivity.

It is possible to make your home a protective tower, even if you live in a basement apartment filled with roommates. Carve out your own space, whether that is your bedroom, a favorite spot to sit, or an entire house—so long as it is yours, and everyone knows it. Mark it as your own magically as well, by drawing a line with salt. Sprinkling just a few grains at a time, create a protective barrier for yourself. If you feel comfortable doing so, you can chant SAFE again and again, hum a song that comforts you, or even just visualize that thorny hedge.

When you're finished, make yourself comfortable behind your salt circle. Notice how it *feels* different. This is real life, so sounds will still intrude. Those around you will still press on your space. But *you* have changed; you have found that inner strength, that barrier that is permeable only to what you allow in. Sweep up the salt, and your barrier remains—it is within you.

pepper berry spritz

Crushed black pepper provides a spicy bite, and blackberries make this boisson bright. In Celtic lore, blackberries are fae fruit and should be eaten with caution—after all, you could be scratched for your trouble. Picking blackberries requires concentration and flexibility, and you must reach carefully, twisting your body to avoid brambles. Sip it on a hot day when the world feels a little oppressive, and it will help you maintain your boundaries.

5 fresh blackberries

1 teaspoon black peppercorns, crushed in a mortar and pestle

1–2 ounces Simple Syrup (see page 10)

Seltzer

Pepper-Infused Vodka (see page 108) (optional)

Muddle the first two ingredients in a shaker, then stir in the Simple Syrup. Add ice and shake it up. Strain into a rocks glass and top with seltzer. Spike with Pepper-Infused Vodka, as desired!

raspberry egg cream

An egg cream is an odd name for a surprising drink. First of all, it contains no eggs and no cream, but it does have milk and seltzer. A chocolate egg cream—the most common variety—is sort of like a sparkling chocolate milk. This raspberry egg cream is both tart and sweet, and its refreshing yet comforting flavor provides you with a blanket of protection.

2 ounces Raspberry Simple Syrup (see page 25)

5 ounces whole milk (substitute almond or oat milk, as desired)

10 ounces seltzer

Mix the raspberry syrup and milk together in a collins glass. Add ice and top with seltzer.

parsley gin rickey

A gin rickey is about as summery as a drink can get. It's simple and tart but with a distinct bite—in this drink, the flavor of the gin is brought forward, and the parsley is sharp and clean. Parsley is a powerful herb; it provides antioxidants and vitamins, aids in digestion, and can lower blood sugar. What it does for your body, it also does for your spirit, giving you a boost of strength and vitality.

A sprig of parsley

1 ounce Protective Lemon Parsley Shrub (see page 105)

¼ teaspoon Bitters for Protection (see page 104)

2 ounces gin

Seltzer

Tear off a handful of parsley and place at the bottom of a collins glass. Add the shrub and bitters, then muddle. Add the gin and ice, then top with seltzer.

bloody mary

Bloody Mary recipes can vary from place to place. Some people like to add horseradish, others beef broth or clam juice (don't knock it till you've tried it). Feel free to experiment with your own classic brunch potion, but this recipe will give you a good place to start.

6 ounces tomato juice

2 dashes (¼ teaspoon) Worcestershire sauce

4 dashes (½ teaspoon) Tabasco sauce

½ ounce Protective Lemon Parsley Shrub (see page 105)

2 ounces Pepper-Infused Vodka (see page 108)

1 teaspoon horseradish, or to taste

Salt and pepper, to taste

Lemon wedge

1 celery stick

Add the first seven ingredients to a collins glass and stir well. Add ice and garnish with a lemon wedge and a stick of celery. The story is that this drink was named after Mary, Queen of Scots, but it may also recall nights spent clutching at friends, chanting "bloody mary, bloody mary" at the mirror, and being certain something horrible would lash out and get us—and yet, we were also certain we would be fine because we had each other. This drink embodies and encourages that certainty—that protection of being among friends.

WISDOM

WHAT IS WISDOM, ANYWAY? IS IT SOMETHING anyone really has? Or is it only found in hindsight?

We strive for wisdom, but all it really means is discernment. It means thinking carefully, considering a situation from all angles, and trying to make the best possible choice we can. We can never really know if we've made the right pick or not—even with hindsight, we know only the one path. Perhaps another choice would have been better . . . but perhaps not.

So it may be that "wisdom" isn't really what this section is after. Instead, perhaps we need to redefine what we mean by it and think of it as taking our time—pondering, considering, and being thoughtful. We will never have all the answers, because there's no cheat sheet at the back of the book of life. But what we can have is faith in ourselves to make the right choices.

We can support this kind of thoughtfulness with rosemary, sage, cinnamon, apple, lime, oak, blueberries, and blackberries. Crystals like amethyst, lapis lazuli, and clear quartz will come to our aid as well.

bitters for wisdom

Legend has it that rosemary grows well in the gardens of strong-willed women—but perhaps it is the other way around? Perhaps rosemary, also known as Compass Leaf, can help you find your path when you feel lost.

1 orange

1 teaspoon dried rosemary

¼ cup vodka

Start by peeling half an orange. Roast the rinds in an oven at 200°F for an hour. Place them in a jar with the dried rosemary and cover with the vodka. Close the jar tightly and let your tincture rest in a cool, dry place for two weeks. Place some clear quartz or amethyst nearby, and let their clarifying energy move through the glass, infusing your bitters with their insight. Give your tincture a gentle shake from time to time, whenever the thought occurs to you.

wise blueberry shrub

Blueberries are connected to the third eye chakra; they allow us to see clearly, not just with our eyes, but with our intuition.

¼ cup blueberries

¼ cup sugar

¼ cup apple cider vinegar

Add a quarter cup of fresh blueberries to a jar and cover them with the sugar. Muddle them a little, popping the berries and releasing their juices. Allow the mixture to steep for one hour, placing a lapis lazuli or other crystal for wisdom nearby. Add the apple cider vinegar, and let your shrub rest on the counter for three days. You may consider pressing your lapis to your third eye, and then placing it atop the jar, making sure that any wisdom you receive from this shrub comes from within *you* and no one else.

On the morning of the fourth day, strain your blue shrub.

cinnamon-infused vodka

Cinnamon has a variety of health benefits. It stimulates the circulatory system, lowers blood sugar, and because it contains high quantities of manganese, it actually improves brain performance as well. Simply smelling cinnamon can improve brain function—it literally makes you wiser.

3 cinnamon sticks

4 cups vodka

Place the cinnamon sticks in a jar and cover them with the vodka. Let it steep in a cool, dark place, surrounded by crystals chosen for wisdom, for three to seven days, tasting it occasionally to see when it reaches the flavor you want—and the level of wisdom you desire. (Is there ever really a limit?)

blueberry sage kombucha

If you only use one herb for wisdom, let it be sage. It is a wisewoman in plant form, able to clear your mind and energy, helping you find that open, thoughtful consideration necessary for true wisdom. That openness is supported by blueberries, which can boost your strength and keep you on your path.

1 batch Basic Kombucha (see page 12)

1 cup blueberries, fresh or frozen

Handful of sage leaves, roughly chopped

At Step 1 of the Basic Kombucha process described on page 13, decant 7 cups of kombucha into a jar or jars, leaving some room at the top. Add the fresh or frozen blueberries and fresh sage leaves, roughly chopped. Seal the jar well, and shake it gently. Let your potion steep in the refrigerator for one week, fermenting and developing its flavor and sparkle.

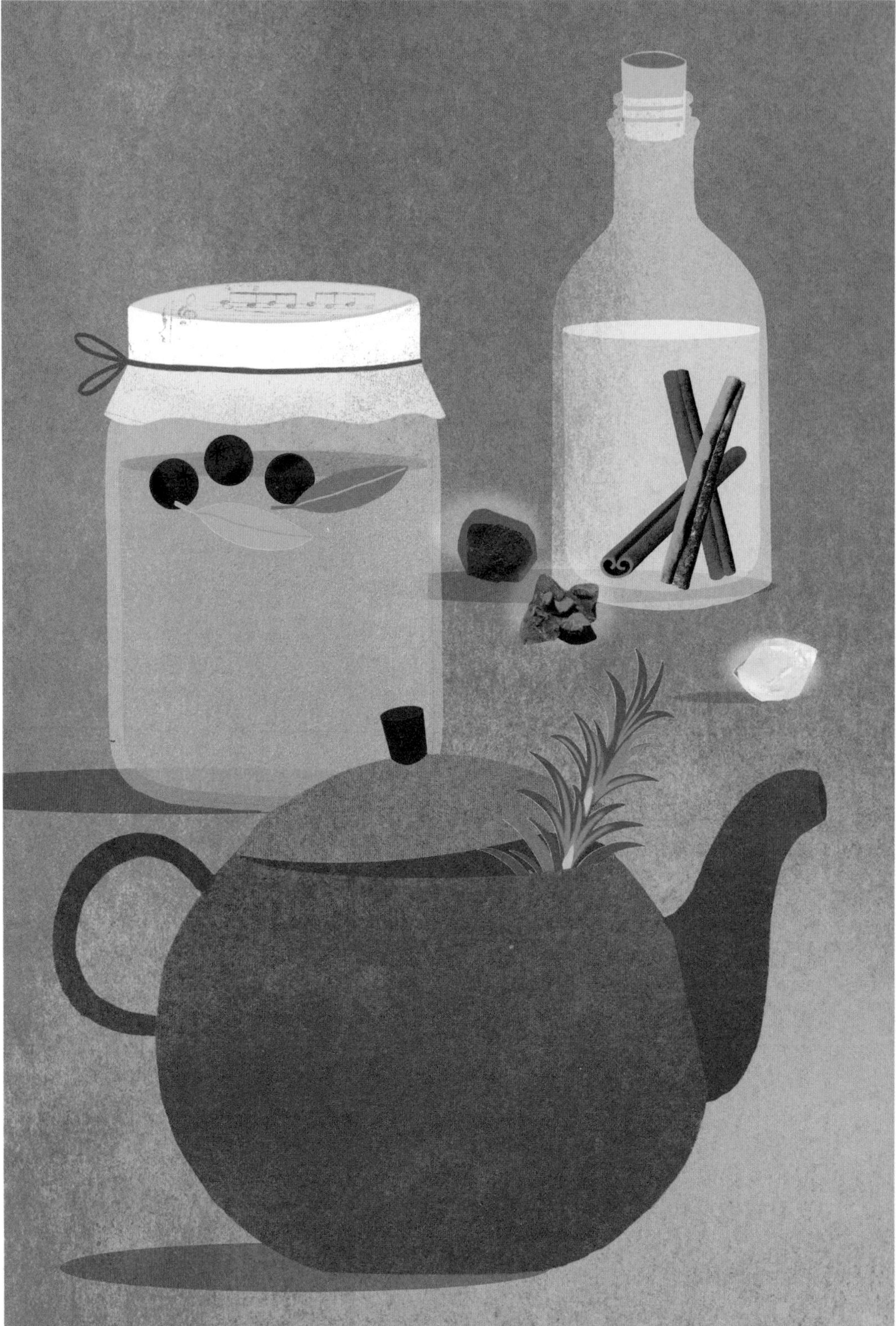

WISDOM TISANE RITUAL

Rosemary is for remembrance.

We cannot really be wise without considering all that has come before, and yet so often we repeat the same mistakes: We fall in love with yet another commitment-phobe. We get into the same argument with our mothers. We wait around for that friend who is always late. And we do it all even though we know better.

The truth is it is hard to keep in mind all the choices we have made. We tend to view each moment anew, reacting to what's in front of us rather than responding to the past. But if we can work to remember what we have done before, we can make different choices. This requires some attention and effort—it's so much easier just to react in the moment. It's a practice to draw on your own wisdom, but one that is so very rewarding.

This tea ritual can help you with that practice, and over time you will get into the habit of remembering and reflecting. It will get easier.

Place a teaspoon of dried rosemary into a strainer. When your water is ready, let the bubbles come to rest before pouring your tea. You don't want to be agitated in this moment. Cover your cup with a small plate and let it steep for 5–10 minutes. While you're waiting, get out your journal. What choice are you pondering right now? There's no need to come up with the answer this second—all you need to do is write down the question.

Take your tea to a comfortable, quiet place. As you sip, write down moments when you have faced this choice before. What did you do? What was the outcome? And now, what are other choices you could make? Consider carefully what their outcomes might be. You can't know for sure, but you *do* know the result of your previous choices. Draw on the magic of your own innate wisdom. What will you do this time?

MEDITATION FOR WISDOM

Find a comfortable seat in a position you can hold for several minutes. Listen to the sounds you hear. Maybe there is someone talking in the next room or a bird singing outside. Close your eyes and allow your breath to deepen. Feel your rib cage expand in all four directions with each inhale and collapse protectively around your heart with each exhale. Bring your attention to each part of your body that is touching the floor, then notice your hands, wherever they are resting. If your palms are facing down, flip them over so they are open and receptive. You may want to hold a crystal for wisdom in your nondominant hand. Notice your spine, and see if you can gently straighten it, letting it reach toward the earth and the sky. Hold your belly in just a little, activating your core, and feeling the power that you carry within you. This is your body. This is your external experience.

Next, move to your internal experience. What emotions can you feel? What thoughts are coming to mind? At the moment, there's no need to try and *avoid* thought; instead, simply pay attention. You might have some song lyrics stuck in your head, or you may be worrying about a task left undone, or you might be going over a conversation in your mind. Become aware of your thoughts.

And now, let them go. They are just thoughts, and they aren't *you*. Let them drift through your mind and leave as easily as they arrived. Pay attention to the space between them, as you pay attention to the space between each inhale and exhale. Feel who you are in the space between.

When you're ready, open your eyes. That space, that open, unencumbered self, is the source of your wisdom. Finding her can help you know how to move forward with care and attention.

apple-sage spritz

An apple plucked from the Tree of Life gave wisdom. Certainly there was a cost, but it's difficult not to feel that it has been worth it in the end. Wisdom is sometimes unpleasant at first, and certainly hard-earned, but the benefits definitely outweigh the losses. That said, this rendition of a wise apple isn't remotely unpleasant—it's warm yet refreshing, and sweet through and through. Let these attributes infuse you as they encourage the introspection that leads to insight.

4 ounces apple cider

2 ounces Blueberry Sage Kombucha (see page 121)

Sage leaf

Bourbon or applejack (optional)

Set up a collins glass with ice and add the cider and kombucha. Garnish with the sage leaf. If you want, you can spike this with some bourbon or applejack.

glögg

Glögg is a Nordic mulled wine, heady and laced with spices, fruits, nuts, and plenty of alcohol. It's best enjoyed around a fire near the Winter Solstice, as you reflect with friends and family on what you would like to know and learn in the year to come, setting your intention that will then draw what you seek from the universe.

1 750 ml bottle oaked red wine

⅓ cup raisins, plus more for garnish

⅓ cup sliced almonds, plus more for garnish

Peel from 1 orange

5 cardamom pods, crushed

5 whole cloves

1 cinnamon stick

4 ounces Cinnamon-Infused Vodka (see page 120)

3 ounces Simple Syrup (see page 10)

Add the first seven ingredients to a large container with a lid. Let it sit for 24 hours at room temperature, then strain into a saucepan. Add the Cinnamon-Infused Vodka and Simple Syrup and bring to just below a simmer—hot enough to serve without cooking off the alcohol. Serve in mugs, garnishing with additional raisins and almonds.

blueberry-rosemary sparkle

This boisson goes heavy on the blueberry, but without being too sweet—it's perfect for the end of summer, when the blueberries are falling off the bushes but you're ready for that bite that comes with the wisdom of fall.

¼ cup fresh blueberries

1–2 ounces Wise Blueberry Shrub (see page 119), to taste

¼ teaspoon Bitters for Wisdom (see page 118)

Seltzer

Vodka (optional)

Muddle the first three ingredients at the bottom of a collins glass, then add ice and top with seltzer. If it's too tart, add more shrub. And you can spike it with vodka, as desired! Enjoy this boisson whenever you feel the need to let your internal wisdom unfold.

blackberry sage

Blackberries and sage work so well together. The tartness of the blackberries balances the earthy herbal flavor of the sage, and when we include the wisdom of a double-oaked whiskey, this potion becomes a very powerful agent for clarity indeed.

5 fresh blackberries

Small handful of fresh sage leaves, torn

½ ounce Simple Syrup (see page 10)

2 ounces double-oaked whiskey like Woodford Reserve

Splash of seltzer

Sage leaf, for garnish

Muddle the first three ingredients in the bottom of a shaker. Add the whiskey and ice and shake well. Strain into a coupe glass, top with seltzer, and garnish with a sage leaf.

INTUITION

IF WISDOM COMES THROUGH THOUGHT AND experience, intuition comes from somewhere else; it emerges from the part of us that connects with *something more*, whether that is God, Source, the Universe, our ancestors, or something personal to your path—it is *your* magic, your insight that perhaps you can't explain, but is always true for you.

Of course, we often spend so much of our lives ignoring our intuition that it becomes hard to hear. This isn't because we don't trust it or ourselves; it's, frankly, that sometimes life just doesn't work that way. You can have a sense that you shouldn't go to work—that something will go wrong and you really ought to stay home today—but unfortunately that's not considered a good excuse for taking an unscheduled vacation day. And so you do go to the office, and something *does* go wrong. Your intuition was right, and it wasn't that you weren't listening—but you just couldn't follow its guidance.

This happens over and over, and eventually we stop bothering to listen to our intuition at all. And that's a shame, because just as often we *can* follow its guidance. We can stay in instead of going out with friends or accept that blind date suggestion even if, most of the time, the night will be disastrous. It's important to boost the volume on your intuition, even if you can't always listen. Calendula, mugwort, lavender, yarrow, lime, apples, cherry, anise, and juniper can all help with this, as can crystals like amazonite, amethyst, lapis lazuli, calcite, opal, and sugilite.

intuitive calendula shrub

The bright orange globes of calendula (also known as marigold) follow the sun as it moves across the sky. Allow these little flower-suns to help you see the light even in the darkest moments, bringing positivity and insight.

1 lime, thinly sliced

¼ cup sugar

¼ cup white wine vinegar

2 tablespoons dried calendula

Slice one lime thinly, then place the slices in a jar. Sprinkle the sugar over them, then close the jar and shake it, coating each lime slice with sugar. Set the jar to rest on a counter. Surround it with your crystals for intuition, placing them in a grid so that their energies can come into vibration with one another. After an hour, add the quarter cup of white wine vinegar and the dried calendula.

Let your potion rest for three days and three nights, giving it a swirl from time to time, and resetting your crystal grid as need be. On the morning of the fourth day, strain out the liquid, and it's ready for your use.

lime-infused gin

Lime has a surprising clarity—more so than lemon, orange, or the other citrus fruits we usually enjoy. When paired with the piney juniper essence found in gin, lime can spark your intuition, allowing you to see clearly when the path forward feels murky.

4 limes, thinly sliced

4 cups gin

Thinly slice four fresh limes. Add them to a jar, and cover them with the gin. Let this steep in a cool, dark place, surrounded by your chosen crystals for intuition, for three to seven days—make sure to start tasting on the third day, as you may prefer your gin more or less limey.

intuitive bitters

These bitters have a complex, herby flavor—there is no citrus element to balance it, so the result is indeed quite bitter. But that is why this tincture is so effective—because it is so potent.

½ teaspoon dried mugwort

½ teaspoon dried lavender

½ teaspoon dried juniper berries

½ teaspoon dried calendula

¼ cup vodka

Place the dried herbs in a small jar. Cover them with the quarter cup of vodka and let the jar rest in a cool, dark place for two weeks. When you place your jar in its spot, take the time to add at least one crystal for intuition (see pages 5–6). Touch your crystal to your mouth and let it feel your breath, and then move it around your head, through your crown chakra—your physical connection with the spiritual world. Touch it to your mouth once more, and then place it beside your tincture. It will help you hear your intuition speak, so that you and others can listen to it.

Repeat this ritual a few times over the course of the next two weeks, and take a moment to give your tincture a gentle swirl or shake to keep the flavors blended.

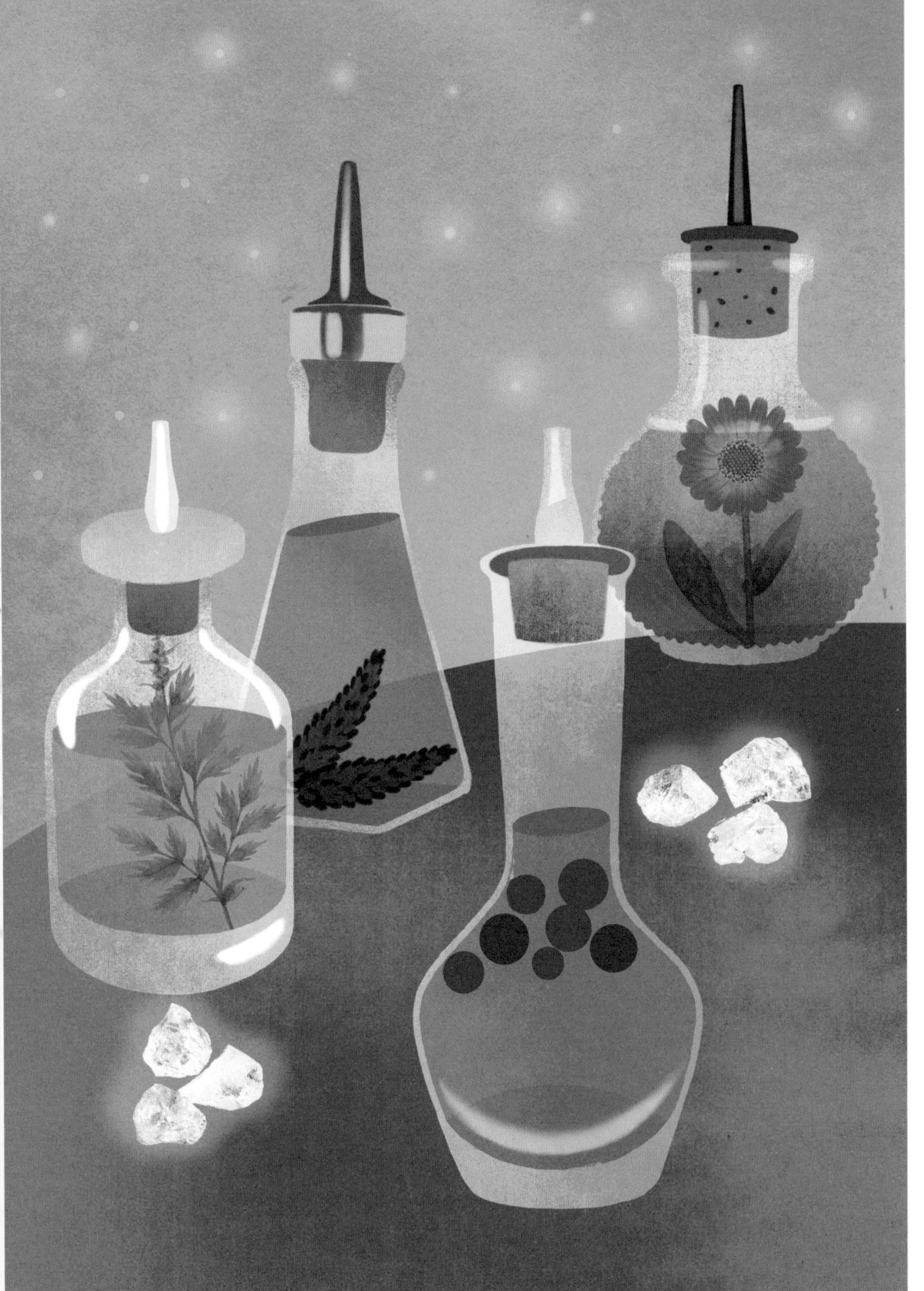

apple kombucha

Apples are a traditional gift to ancestors or spirits on the other side of the veil. They are an offering, given freely, but also shared in the hope that their recipient will be inclined to offer some guidance. Apples can serve as a bridge between this world and another, more mysterious one.

1 batch Basic Kombucha (see page 12)

1 apple, cored and cubed

1 cup natural apple juice or apple cider

At Step 1 of the Basic Kombucha process described on page 13, decant 7 cups of kombucha into a jar or jars, leaving some room at the top. Core and cube one apple and add it to your kombucha, followed by a cup of natural apple juice or apple cider, depending on what's available. Seal the jar well, and shake it gently. Let it steep in the refrigerator for one week, and then enjoy to enhance connection to the greater collective.

intuitive tisane

Prepare this tisane at night—it doesn't contain any caffeine or other energy-boosters, and it will help to invite dreams. Often our dreams are trying to communicate something, whether that is a message from outside ourselves or something we already know, deep down.

1 teaspoon mixed dried herbs (lavender, yarrow, calendula)

Honey, to taste

Milk, to taste

Collect a teaspoon's worth of dried lavender, yarrow, and calendula. Put your mixture in a tea strainer, and pour some just-boiled water over it. Cover your mug and allow it to steep for 5–10 minutes. Stir in some honey and milk; you want this to be a soothing and comforting experience. Enjoy your tea in a dimly lit room; you can light candles or simply keep on a low lamp. If you want, and if it's bright enough to see, you can sketch or journal, or simply sip your brew thoughtfully. Spend this time considering the events of the day. Is there anything that requires additional reflection? Did something annoying happen, and the best thing to do is let it go? Did something amazing happen, and you want to make sure you don't forget the experience?

When you've finished your tea, prepare for bed, moving slowly through your nighttime ritual. Close your eyes and allow sleep to come, bringing with it whatever your dreams have to tell you.

MOON RITUAL FOR INTUITION

If the sun shows us what can clearly be seen, the moon can help us see with our third eye, as we access the unseen. On the night of the full moon, find a place where you can be bathed in her light. If you can go outdoors, wonderful, but light coming through a window will work just as well. Fill a bowl, ideally a glass or ceramic one, with water—you just want it to feel as close to natural as possible. Place your bowl of water where the moonlight falls, blessing it.

Move your hands over the bowl, letting the moonlight bless your palms. Move them up to your face, transferring her blessing. Sit back and close your eyes. What is it you wish to know? Perhaps you are seeking messages from your ancestors, or perhaps you simply want to feel a connection with *something more*. If there is something specific you desire, focus on it, but remain open to whatever comes.

Lean forward and peer into the bowl. Let your gaze go a little out of focus, and notice anything you see. Perhaps there are tiny ripples in the water, caused by your breath or the vibrations of the world around you. Do you see anything in the water? Do you imagine seeing something in the water? Both are correct, and both come from your intuition and your spell. This is a deep magical practice called scrying, and it is allowing you to come into contact with the most ancient parts of yourself, and of the world.

When you have finished scrying, and feel that you have seen all that you are meant to, you can use your moon-charged water to cleanse your crystals (making sure in advance they can be safely placed in water) or to make a simple syrup.

dark and stormy

Could there be a drink with a witchier name? The Dark and Stormy cocktail originates from the Caribbean in sailor and pirating times, when all you needed was a bottle of rum and whatever else was on hand. As it turns out, a Dark and Stormy doesn't actually need *rum—it's delicious anyway! And despite its name, it is a clear, far-seeing beverage, which allows you to peer through the storms and the darkness to whatever lies on the other side.*

7½ ounces ginger beer

Juice of 1 lime

⅛ teaspoon Intuitive Bitters (see page 134)

Dark rum, to taste (optional)

Mix all the ingredients together over ice in a collins glass. And of course, you can always add a splash (or two!) of dark rum.

clear-eyed gimlet

There's a theory that this cocktail was also created by sailors of yore, who in addition to their daily ration of liquor, needed some vitamin C to stave off scurvy. Or perhaps they were using the intuitive powers of gin and lime to aid them in navigating rough seas. Either way, a gimlet will help you do the same. Enjoy this drink when you need to see with a clearer third eye.

2½ ounces Lime-Infused Gin (see page 133)

½ ounce Simple Syrup (see page 10)

Squeeze of fresh lime

Lime slice

Add the first three ingredients to a cocktail shaker filled with ice and shake well. Strain into a martini glass and serve with a thin slice of lime.

cherry temple

Historically, cherries have often been used for divination—and what is divination but learning to listen to the sound of something more? *They are also, of course, delicious, but working them into a drink can be a little labor-intensive. It's worth it, though! If you can find fresh pitted cherries, you'll save yourself some work, but there's something pleasurable about cutting up some cherries. Again, if you have a cherry pitter, great, but otherwise a paring knife will do.*

This recipe is inspired by the Shirley Temple, the drink we were allowed to order on special occasions when the adults were having cocktails. Sweetened with grenadine syrup and always garnished with at least one maraschino cherry, they often taste overly sweet and syrupy to a grown-up palate. This more refreshing spin employs kombucha for sparkle and actual fresh cherries, helping to bridge the natural intuition of childhood and bring it to a place you can find it today.

3–4 fresh cherries, pitted

1 teaspoon Intuitive Calendula Shrub (see page 132)

1–2 cups Apple Kombucha (see page 136)

1 stemmed cherry

Muddle the fresh cherries with the shrub at the bottom of a collins glass, then add ice and top with kombucha. Garnish with a stemmed cherry, and be sure to tie knots in the stem, just like when you were small.

sazerac

The Sazerac is one of several classic drinks from New Orleans—arguably the most magical place in the United States—and if there's a Venn diagram for magic and cocktails, New Orleans is definitely at the center. A traditional Sazerac contains two kinds of bitters, sugar, and a splash of absinthe—not enough to give you visions, but plenty to open up your third eye, allowing your intuition to see more clearly. To be true to this cocktail, this recipe does not call for homemade bitters, but you can substitute the commercial bitters for Creativity Bitters and Bitters for Growth, respectively.

Splash of absinthe or Herbsaint

1 teaspoon sugar

2 dashes (¼ teaspoon) Peychaud's Bitters or Creativity Bitters (see page 18)

2 dashes (¼ teaspoon) Angostura bitters or Bitters for Growth (see page 146)

2 ounces rye whiskey

Twist of lemon

Pour just a touch of absinthe into a rocks glass. Swirl it around so the entire glass is coated, then pour out whatever is left. Add the sugar and both bitters, and muddle them together to create a slurry. Add the whiskey and two or three ice cubes. Stir well to chill the drink and meld the flavors. Add the lemon twist and serve.

As you take your first sips, close your eyes and try to taste all the individual flavors. See if you can pull them apart. If there's a certain flavor that draws your attention, indulge that instinct. What is it trying to tell you?

GROWTH

EVERY SECTION IN THIS BOOK HAS BEEN leading to this one—for what is it we are striving for if not growth? It's what we do throughout our lives, stretching for who we are meant to be as a vine stretches for the sun. We need courage and creativity, love and protection, calm, balance, and harmony, and most of all wisdom and intuition—all of these support us in our growth and help us get there.

But where is "there" exactly? There is no end point. There is no finish line for growth—we are always growing, always striving, always becoming more than we were before. It's our right and privilege in this life, and every day takes us forward.

This isn't to say that growth is always easy or enjoyable. Some of the hardest things in life bring the most growth, like the pruning of a tree. But there is so much that nature has to offer that can support us, hold us up when we fall, or comfort us when the pains of our development become difficult to bear. Cinnamon, anise, rosemary, mint, ginger, agave, rice, watermelon, and all citrus including lemon, lime, orange, and grapefruit are here to light your way. The warm vibrations of pyrite, peridot, yellow jasper, and aventurine will also resonate you, helping you feel certain that yes, this is the right path.

bitters for growth

These bitters are warm and spicy, offset by a light orange flavor.

1 orange, peeled

1 star anise

1 cinnamon stick

¼ cup vodka

Start by peeling half an orange. Roast the rinds in an oven at 200°F for an hour, then place them in a small jar. Add the star anise and cinnamon stick, then cover with a quarter cup of vodka. Let the jar rest in a cool, dark place for two weeks. If you can, clear a bit of space around it, making room for a circle of crystals. Give the energy of your tincture room to grow.

Over the course of the next two weeks, visit your tincture from time to time, offering it the same love and support it will give to you.

lemon lime shrub

This shrub combines the flavors of lemon and lime and uses rice vinegar instead of plain white vinegar. The flavor becomes a subtle, sweet citrus, leaning neither toward lemon nor lime, but resting somehow in between.

½ lime, thinly sliced

½ lemon, thinly sliced

¼ cup sugar

¼ cup rice vinegar

Slice half a lime thinly, then place the slices in a jar. Repeat with half a lemon. Sprinkle a quarter cup of sugar over your fruit, then close the jar and shake it, coating each slice with sugar. Place the jar on the counter, and rest pyrite atop it, to help it stay grounded, and put aventurine and yellow jasper on either side, to help it grow. After an hour, add the rice vinegar. Let your potion steep for three days and three nights, giving it a swirl from time to time and checking the placement of your crystals. On the morning of the fourth day, strain out the liquid, as it's ready for your use.

all the citrus kombucha

This kombucha takes the growth-boosting properties of citrus and packs them all in! The recipe includes citrus fruits commonly available at grocery stores, but if you have access to yuzu, tangerine, or anything else, definitely add it in! The idea here is to pack in everything you can—all the growth-inducing flavors—creating one marvelous burst of forward momentum.

1 batch Basic Kombucha (see page 12)

Half an orange, sliced

Half a grapefruit, sliced

1 lemon, sliced

1 lime, sliced

At Step 1 of the Basic Kombucha process described on page 13, decant 7 cups of kombucha into a jar or jars, leaving some room at the top. Add the remaining ingredients to the decanted kombucha. Seal the jar well, and shake it gently. Let it steep in the refrigerator for one week, and then enjoy as needed with the intention of nurturing who you are meant to be!

ginger-infused vodka

The spice of ginger is like a wake-up call to the senses. It is somehow warm yet cool, with a bite that is sharp and still refreshing. If you're feeling stagnant, stuck, and not moving forward, ginger can give you the boost you need to kick-start progress.

4-inch piece of ginger, peeled and thinly sliced

4 cups vodka

Peel and thinly slice a 4-inch piece of fresh ginger, then put the slices in a jar. Cover with the vodka. Let it steep in a cool, dark place, surrounded by crystals you've chosen to nurture growth, for three to seven days. Taste it on the third day, but you may well decide to let it steep longer.

sun tea

Nothing supports growth like the sun. Sun tea is made by using the heat of the sun to slowly brew your tea; it's like a warm brew, rather than the hot brew you get from boiling water from the stove. You can use standard tea bags for this or create your own mix of herbal tea. You can use one of the recipes from this book or craft a blend of your very own. What will best support your growth?

Since it takes a while, sun tea is generally made in batches, rather than just a cup at a time, so you'll need a very large glass jar or dispenser, enough to hold a gallon of tea. Of course, if you want to make less, just cut down on the recipe.

8 tea bags, or 8 teaspoons' worth of herbs placed in tea strainers or tied off in cheesecloth

Honey, agave syrup, or Simple Syrup (see page 10), to taste

Lemon slices

Add 1 gallon of water to your jar and place your tea bags in it. Let your tea steep for at least two to three hours in direct sunlight. Give it a taste to see if it is strong enough—if not, let it sit longer. When it's ready, you can add honey, agave syrup, or Simple Syrup to the jar and pop in some slices of lemon. Serve over ice, and let this sun-brewed iced tea warm your soul and cool your body, all at the same time.

RITUAL FOR GROWTH

The natural world can give us all the inspiration for growth we need, teaching us that it must move in two directions—upward toward the sun and also downward into the earth. We must stay grounded in what supports us and matters to us most—our families, friends, and a sense of peace and safety. But we must also always reach upward, stretching for love, creativity, and a connection with *something more*.

First, choose the time of day that is right for the growth you want to encourage in yourself. You could get up with the dawn to support a new beginning. You could stand in the brightest sun at high noon, feeling your most powerful. You could perform this ritual at dusk, when the veil between worlds is thin, allowing you to receive messages you might not otherwise be able to hear.

If you can manage it, try to be outside for this ritual. You will need a patch of earth, so find a garden if you can, but you can also use a potted plant in your house to evoke the connection to Mother Earth. You'll need a piece of paper, a pen or pencil, and a tincture. You can use the Bitters for Growth on page 146, or choose any other of the tinctures included in this book if you're looking to nurture something specific. This is your spell, and you get to design it.

When the time and place feel right to you, use your chosen tincture to anoint yourself on the top of your head, your third eye, your throat, your heart space, your solar plexus, your lower back, and the base of your spine. You can do this either by rubbing a drop of the tincture into your skin or simply by rubbing a drop between your thumb and index finger held right above the space in question—whichever you choose, your chakra will be stimulated. Close your eyes and stand tall, bringing your chakras into alignment, straight up and down, and stretching between the earth and the sky. Feel your feet rooted into the earth, as if two ropes were pulling down through your arches, anchoring you. At the same time, feel your heart lift toward the sky, as if filled with helium. Feel a third string pulling from the top of your head, raising you up. Somehow, you are not being pulled apart. These are opposing forces, but all are supporting you.

Keeping your eyes closed, lift your nondominant foot and place it on the ground so that its heel is perpendicular to your standing foot. Lift your standing foot and bring your feet back to parallel—you've made something like a 45-degree turn. Repeat these steps, turning until you feel like you've come back to the beginning. Don't open your eyes, but begin the turn going the other way, lifting the opposite foot first. Step and turn all the way around until you feel you've come back to the beginning once more.

Now open your eyes.

You aren't back where you started—not exactly.

Every step we take is a journey that brings us somewhere new, and that is *always* true, even when we feel like we are repeating the same mistakes or simply living the same day over and over. We are always growing, always changing.

Knowing that you are always growing and moving forward, how can you choose to do so with intention? How can you direct your growth so that you will be happiest? Most peaceful? Most fulfilled? Take a piece of paper and write a question, a mantra, a goal, or even just a word that supports you. Fold it in half, and in half again. Use your fingers (first checking to make sure the dirt is free of glass or other contaminants, of course) to dig a small hole in the earth. Place your paper in the earth, and cover it back up again. It will be there, held by Mama Earth, supporting you as you grow.

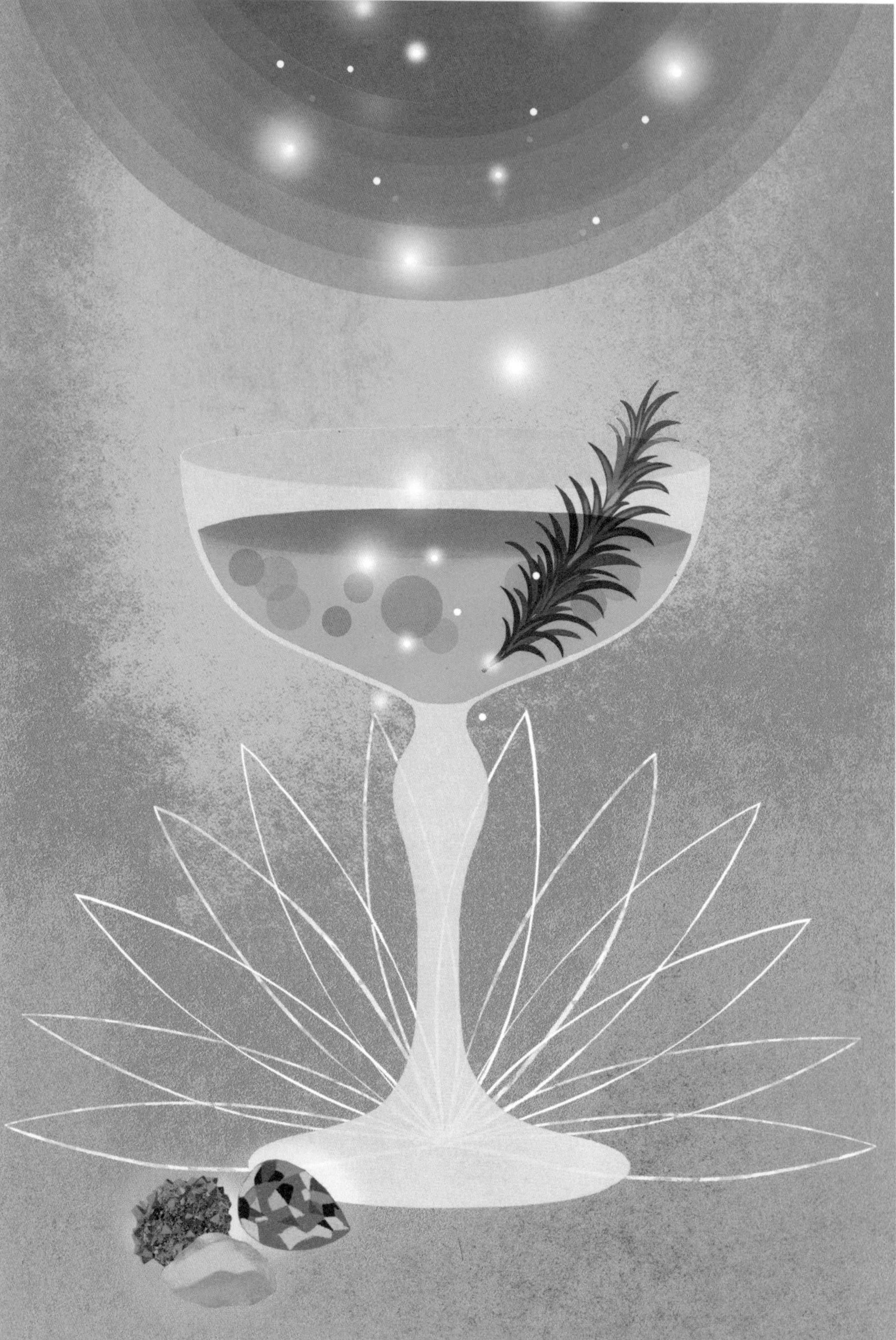

agave-grapefruit spritz

If we are to be inspired by growth in nature, perhaps nothing is more impressive than the agave plant. They grow extremely slowly, in the most arid of conditions—but they do grow. And when they flower, their stalk or "mast" can grow up to 40 feet high. This potion uses two different spirits crafted from agave—tequila and mezcal. It is quite potent, so before you drink it, be mindful of setting your intentions for the kind of growth you want. It wouldn't do to sprout 40 feet in the wrong direction.

1 ounce tequila

2 ounces mezcal

4 ounces grapefruit soda

A sprig of rosemary

In a rocks glass, combine the tequila and mezcal. Add ice and top with the grapefruit soda. Garnish with a sprig of rosemary.

grapefruit spritz

Inspired by a Greyhound, this sweeter, more cheerful boisson invokes a late spring day, when the leaves on the trees have finished opening but are still pale green, with that waxy tenderness of texture. This is the kind of growth that we already know will be successful, but is still in its first flush. It's a state we can all bask in.

FOR THE SIMPLE SYRUP:

1 grapefruit, zested then juiced

1 cup sugar

FOR THE DRINK:

½ ounce Grapefruit Simple Syrup

1 dash (⅛ teaspoon) Bitters for Growth (see page 146)

1 ounce Lemon Lime Shrub (see page 147)

All the Citrus Kombucha (see page 148)

Vodka (optional)

Start by making the Grapefruit Simple Syrup, combining the juice and zest of a grapefruit—should be about a cup's worth of juice—with the cup of sugar. Heat in a saucepan on low for 20 minutes, then strain.

In a collins glass, combine half an ounce of Grapefruit Simple Syrup, the Bitters for Growth, and the Lemon Lime Shrub. Stir them together, then add ice and top with the All the Citrus Kombucha. Spike with vodka, as desired.

watermelon refresh

This drink is perfect for those summer days when you've spotted a giant watermelon in the grocery store and felt you absolutely had to have it. *But then you got it home, and, well, that's a lot of watermelon. After a day or two, it's a little soft and overripe.*

1 watermelon, peeled and cut into chunks

Juice of half a lime

A sprig of mint

Rum (optional)

Once your watermelon has reached the point of nearly being overripe, cut it up into chunks as best you can and toss them into a blender. Add the juice of half a lime (you may need more, depending on how much watermelon you're juicing), and blend it up.

Garnish with a sprig of mint, and feel free to add some white rum, as desired. Incidentally, this is also excellent poured into a popsicle mold and frozen for later, calling back to childhood, when growth was a given and not something we needed to keep striving for. This boisson, whether in liquid or solid form, is a reminder that we *do* continue to grow, and that it can be easy and fun.

ginger saketini

Most saketinis tend to be overly sweet, drenched in vermouth, fruit syrups, or both. But they don't have to be, and this particular saketini is clear and refreshing. The wake-up call of the ginger is there, but it doesn't overwhelm the delicate flavor of the rice wine. This is a balanced, thoughtful growth, like a vine that reaches forward carefully—gingerly even—for the support that it needs.

1 ounce Ginger-Infused Vodka (see page 150)

2 ounces mild sake

Cucumber slice

In an ice-filled shaker, combine the Ginger-Infused Vodka and a smooth, mild sake, like junmai ginjo. Shake well, then strain into a martini glass. Garnish with a slice of cucumber.

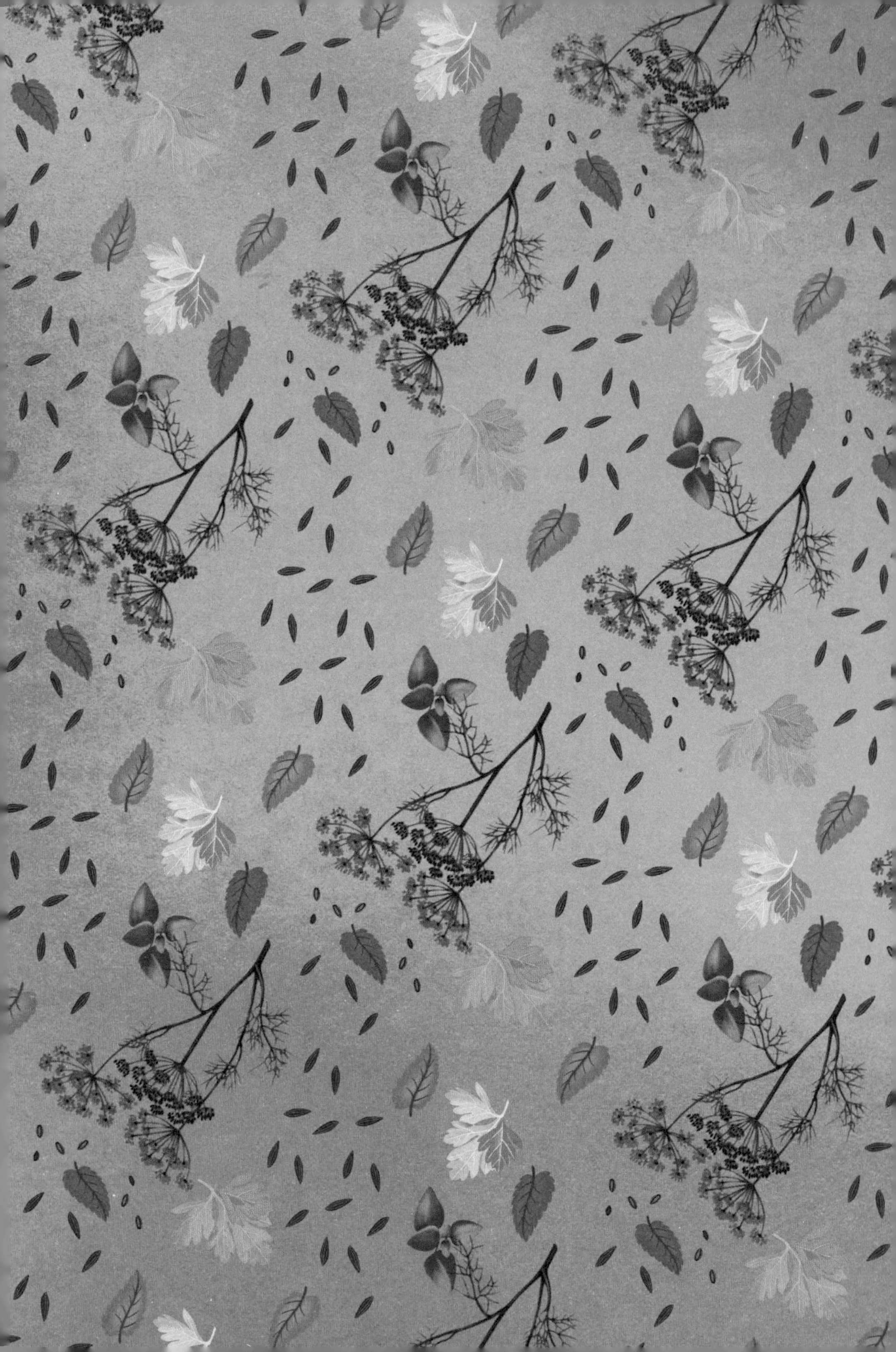

CONCLUSION

THE RECIPES HERE ARE SAMPLES OF POTIONS that can get you started on crafting your own, allowing you to experiment with flavors and attributes. Perhaps at the end of a long day you want to mix a cocktail for calm and intuition, so that you have a sleep filled with dreams—in which case, you might want to make something with calendula, lavender, and gin. Or maybe it's a lazy Saturday afternoon, and you want to get some energy together to create something. So you brew up a potion using raspberries, mint, and lemon.

You know what you need, and you have all that you require to make it. But potion-brewing is just one of many ways to manifest magic in the world. You can take the skills and knowledge you've acquired and bring them into the rest of your life, whether that means crafting your own soaps and lotions, performing daily rituals, creating spells, or simply moving through life with intention and awareness of the power that you have and that surrounds you every moment of every day.

acknowledgments

When I came up with the idea of writing this book, I was 90 percent sure someone would point at me and say, "Show me your bartending certification." But I am eternally grateful to Shannon Fabricant for rolling with the creativity and *fun* of these potions, and letting me tinker and brew to my heart's content! I feel like I can never say enough about how wonderful it is to work with her, *and* to work with the amazing Susan Van Horn, who sees things I never would, with an artistry and passion I can only admire. The same admiration must go to Ashley Benning, who goes beyond copyediting (which is already hard enough!) and looks for ways to make every book something more. Amber Morris, you keep everything running so smoothly that from where I sit it looks like magic. Kristin Kiser, Amy Cianfrone, Kara Thornton, Jessica Schmidt, and the entire Running Press team—I am so very grateful for all that you do. Thank you.

Thank you to Anna Godeassi for a stunningly beautiful book. I want to decorate my entire house with your glorious artwork.

Writing this book was a joy. I mean, it's not every day you can make yourself a cocktail and call it work! But it did involve a lot of experimentation, and needed *a lot* of support. My dear Potions Testers, Annie, Hannah, and Puanani—thank you all for your hard work! Thank you to Dave for trying *everything*, to Mom and Dad for trying most things, and to Michael and Victoria for their warm enthusiasm.

But more than anyone, and perhaps surprisingly for a book of cocktails, I have to thank my daughter Maile. An avid potion-maker herself, she helped me craft the majority of the boissons and valiantly tasted every nonalcoholic beverage, providing thoughtful feedback every time. I couldn't have written this book without her.

index